Successful Writing
INTERMEDIATE

Teacher's book

Virginia Evans

Express Publishing

Published by Express Publishing in 2000

Liberty House, New Greenham Park, Newbury,
Berkshire RG19 6HW
Tel.: (0044) 1635 817 363
Fax: (0044) 1635 817 463
e-mail: inquiries@expresspublishing.co.uk
INTERNET http: //www.expresspublishing.co.uk

© Virginia Evans, 2000

Design and Illustration © Express Publishing, 2000

All rights reserved. No part of this publication may be reproduced, stored in a retrieval system, or transmitted in any form, or by any means, electronic, photocopying or otherwise, without the prior written permission of the publishers.

ISBN 1-903128-51-X

Contents

Unit 1	**Part A** - Guidelines for Writing	5
	Part B - Letter writing	8
Unit 2	Informal Letters	9
Unit 3	Formal Letters	12
Unit 4	Semi-formal Letters	16
Unit 5	Transactional Letters	18
Unit 6	Describing People	19
Unit 7	Describing Places/Buildings	23
Unit 8	Describing Objects	27
Unit 9	Describing Festivals/Events/Celebrations	29
Unit 10	First-person Narratives	31
Unit 11	Third-person Narratives	34
Unit 12a	News Reports	36
Unit 12b	Reviews	39
Unit 13	"For and Against" Essays	41
Unit 14a	Opinion Essays	45
Unit 14b	Providing Solutions to Problems	48
Unit 14c	Letters to the Editor	50
Unit 15	Assessment and Proposal Reports	52
Revision Extension Section		56
Tapescripts		74

Abbreviations used in the book

Ex.	=	exercise
HW	=	homework
L1	=	students' first language/mother tongue
mins.	=	minutes
p.	=	page
pp.	=	pages
S	=	student
Ss	=	students
T	=	teacher

Unit 1 Part A Guidelines for Writing (pp. 4 - 15)

1 *(Present the theory and explain the meaning of any unknown terminology. Explain/Elicit the meaning of any unknown vocabulary in the extracts. Ask individual Ss to read the extracts aloud and elicit which type of composition each is from. Allow Ss two or three mins. to complete the task. Check Ss' answers.)*

1 G   2 A   3 E   4 F   5 C   6 D   7 B

2 *(Read the extracts aloud and explain/elicit the meaning of any unknown words. Allow Ss about four mins. to complete the task, then check Ss' answers.)*

1 G   2 C   3 F   4 E   5 D   6 A   7 B

3 *(Read the rubric, ensuring that Ss understand the task. Allow Ss two or three mins. to complete the task, then check Ss' answers around the class.)*

1 reader
2 situation
3 type of writing
4 specific topics

4 *(Read the rubric aloud, then allow Ss three or four mins. to underline the key words and answer the questions. Check Ss' answers around the class.)*

1 My manager.
2 I work for a local tourist office and the manager has asked me to write a report on a new restaurant which has just opened in our town.
3 An assessment report/A report.
4 I should include a description of the restaurant, the food and the service and I should comment on the restaurant's good and bad points.

5 a) *(Read the rubric aloud, then allow Ss three or four mins. to underline the key words and answer the questions. Check Ss' answers around the class.)*

Key words: you are a writer – your editor – short article about famous person – twentieth century – you admire – describing personality – reasons you admire him/her

1 C   2 B   3 B, C, E   4 B, D

b) Johann Strauss, because he lived in the nineteenth century.

6 a) *(Allow Ss two or three mins. to complete the task, then check Ss' answers around the class.)*

why you admire the person
personality

b) *(Allow Ss two or three mins. to complete the task, then check Ss' answers around the class.)*

why you admire the person: helped those in need; entire life was devoted to others; donated money to charity
personality: selfless, compassionate, courageous, patient

7 *(Present the theory and explain the meaning of any unknown terminology. Allow Ss about two mins. to complete the task, then check Ss' answers.)*

a) B   b) A

8 *(Allow Ss three or four mins. to read the article and complete the task. Explain/Elicit the meaning of any words Ss do not understand, then check Ss' answers.)*

Para 1: person's name and reason you chose her
Para 2: personal qualities
Para 3: reasons you admire her
Para 4: final comments/feelings

1 Mother Teresa.
2 She devoted all of her time to others and never put her own needs first. She was also very courageous and never thought of the risks she was taking when looking after people who were sick or dying.
3
- Her entire life was devoted to charity work. For example, she opened a centre in Calcutta for the terminally ill, ... dignity.
- She also won many awards including the Nobel Peace Prize in 1979. She donated all the money from her awards to fund other centres.

9 *(Present the theory, then allow Ss two or three mins. to read the main body paragraphs of the article again. Check Ss' answers by asking individual Ss to report back to the class.)*

Topic sentences
Para 2: Mother Teresa was a selfless person.
(This can be replaced by No 2)
Para 3: What I admire most about Mother Teresa are her achievements.
(This can be replaced by No 1)

Unit 1

10 a) *(Explain/Elicit the meaning of any unknown words. Allow Ss two or three mins. to complete the task, then check Ss' answers.)*

    A 2   B 3

b) *(Read the questions aloud and elicit answers from individual Ss.)*

- They belong to the main body of the composition.
- Banning cars from the city centre.
- A discursive essay (a "for and against" essay).

11 *(Explain/Elicit the meaning of any unknown words. Read the sentences aloud and ask individual Ss to identify the relevant sentences. Check Ss' answers.)*

    A, C

12 *(Allow Ss three or four mins. to think of appropriate supporting sentences. Ask individual Ss to report back to the class.)*

(Suggested answers)
1. He's tall and slim with short, straight, brown hair and brown eyes. He usually wears a suit and tie.
2. She likes being with people and everyone has fun being with her. She enjoys going to parties and never turns down an invitation to an evening out with friends.

13 *(Allow Ss two or three mins. to think of appropriate topic sentences. Ask individual Ss to report back to the class.)*

(Suggested answers)
A Making your own clothes has certain advantages.
B There are certain disadvantages to spending money on medical research.

14 *(Present the theory. Explain/Elicit the meaning of any unknown words and allow Ss two or three mins. to complete the task. Check Ss' answers.)*

2 On the other hand   5 because
3 What is more   6 However
4 As a result

15 *(Read the extract aloud and explain/elicit the meaning of any unknown words. Allow Ss three or four mins. to complete the task, then check Ss' answers.)*

1 As a result   3 On the other hand
2 What is more   4 For example

16 *(Allow Ss two or three mins. to complete the task. Check Ss' answers around the class.)*

1 Simon failed the exam **since** he had not studied enough.
2 **Although** ordering take-away food is very convenient, it can be rather expensive.
3 Aaron wanted to go to the football match **but** his mother wouldn't let him.
4 Adventure holidays can be very tiring **and** (they can be) quite dangerous.
5 It started getting cold **so** I put on a jumper.
6 **Even though** the hairdresser said it was perfectly safe, the chemicals in the dye made my hair turn green.

17 *(Allow Ss two or three mins. to complete the task. Check Ss' answers around the class.)*

1 As   3 despite   5 Even though
2 therefore 4 such as

18 *(Present the theory and explain/elicit the meaning of any unknown words. Allow Ss three or four mins. to identify the writing techniques used. Check Ss' answers.)*

1 rhetorical question
2 addressing the reader directly
3 creating mystery and suspense
4 setting the scene
5 quotation

19 a) *(Explain/Elicit the meaning of any unknown words. Allow Ss three or four mins. to complete the task. Check Ss' answers.)*

A 2   narrative (third person)
B 3   discursive essay (opinion essay)
C 1   description of a person

b) *(Allow Ss two or three mins to read the extracts again and ask individual Ss to identify the writing techniques used in each.)*

Successful Writing Intermediate - Unit 1

quotation	3
proverb/saying	2
addressing the reader directly	B, 1
direct speech	A, C, 2

20 *(Read the extracts aloud and explain/elicit the meaning of any unknown words. Allow Ss about two mins. to complete the task, then check Ss' answers.)*

A 1 impressive 3 comfortable
 2 huge 4 most extraordinary

B 1 whispering 3 peered
 2 paused 4 crept

21 *(Present the theory. Read the phrases aloud and check that Ss understand their meaning. Allow Ss three or four mins. to complete the task, then check Ss' answers.)*

2 am entitled to (formal style)
3 Drop by (informal style)
4 point in favour of (formal style)
5 were seriously injured (formal style)
6 with flying colours (informal style)
7 porcelain-white skin (formal style)
8 To my mind (formal style)
9 Don't miss it! (informal style)
10 won't be able to make it (informal style)

22 *(Read the extracts aloud and explain/elicit the meaning of any unknown words.)*

a) *(Elicit from individual Ss what type of writing each extract is from.)*

A discursive essay (opinion essay)
B formal letter
C informal letter
D (assessment) report
E news report
F narrative (third person)
G semi-formal letter

b) *(Allow Ss about three mins. to complete the task. Check Ss' answers around the class.)*

1 C, E, G 3 C 5 A
2 A, E, F 4 A, B, D

23 *(Read the situations aloud and elicit answers from individual Ss.)*

a F (because you are writing to sb you do not know)
b S - F (because the magazine readers are quite young)
c I (because you are writing to a friend of yours)
d F or S - F (because a news report is a factual piece of writing)
e S - F (because you need to sound polite and respectful to your friends' parents)

24 *(Read the extracts aloud, explain/elicit the meaning of any unknown words, and ensure that Ss understand the task. Elicit answers from individual Ss.)*

A 1 Firstly 4 What is more
 2 was not 5 the slightest
 3 reached 6 collapsed

B 1 really love 4 Also
 2 I've met 5 in common
 3 dull moment

C 1 however 4 computer-generated
 2 full of comical images
 scenes 5 extremely realistic
 3 What is more

25 *(Present the theory, read the extract aloud and explain/elicit the meaning of any unknown words. Allow Ss about four mins. to complete the task. Check Ss' answers by asking individual Ss to read the corrected mistakes aloud.)*

2 runing → running (S)
3 made → threw/gave (WW)
4 better → best (G)
5 america → America (P)
6 successfull → successful (S)
7 such ill → so ill (WW/G)
8 hadn't been able go → hadn't been able to go (G)

26 *(Allow Ss about two mins. to complete the task. Check Ss' answers.)*

A 2 B 1 C 5 D 4 E 3

Unit 1 Part B Letter writing (pp. 16 - 19)

1 *(Present the theory and explain the meaning of any unknown terminology. Explain/Elicit the meaning of any unknown vocabulary in the extracts. Ask individual Ss to read the extracts aloud and elicit which type of letter each is from. Allow Ss two or three mins. to complete the task. Check Ss' asnwers.)*

1 E   2 C   3 A   4 D   5 F   6 B

(Suggested answers)
Key words:
A come to my party
B what you think I should do; I really need your advice
C I'm having a fantastic time; I went sailing; I'm going to take part in
D if you could give me some more information
E if you could consider my application
F I am writing to complain about

2 *(Read the paragraphs aloud and explain/elicit the meaning of any unknown words. Allow Ss about two mins. to complete the task, then check Ss' answer.)*

A 2   B 3   C 1, Letter refusing an invitation

3 *(Present the theory and explain the meaning of any unknown terminology. Ask individual Ss to read the phrases aloud and elicit which phrase is formal and which is informal. Allow Ss two or three mins. to complete the task, then check Ss' answers.)*

1 F	4 F	7 F	10 F	13 I
2 I	5 F	8 F	11 F	14 F
3 F	6 I	9 I	12 I	15 I

4 *(Allow Ss about two mins. to read the situation and complete the task. Then ask individual Ss to report back to the class.)*

a) A informal
    B semi-formal
    C formal

b) 1 C — a friend
   2 A — your former teacher
   3 B — a careers advisor

5 *(Allow Ss about two mins to read the pairs of expressions. Ask individual Ss to identify which expressions are informal and which semi-formal. Allow Ss three or four mins. to complete the task. Then check Ss' answers.)*

a) **Letter A**
1 Hi — just a quick note
2 say thanks a lot
3 all your help
4 getting ready
5 What you did
6 played a big part
7 making sure
8 whole thing
9 went so well
10 thank you enough for

Letter B
1 I am writing
2 thank you very much
3 your kind assistance
4 preparations
5 Your contribution
6 was very important
7 ensuring
8 occasion
9 was such a success
10 tell you how much I appreciate

b) Letter A is informal
   Letter B is semi-formal
   They are letters thanking someone.

6 *(Read aloud the beginnings and endings and elicit any unknown words. Allow Ss two mins. to complete the task, then check Ss' answers.)*

1 C letter giving news; informal style
2 E letter asking for information; formal style
3 D letter accepting an invitation; informal style
4 A letter apologising for sth; informal style
5 F letter of complaint; formal style
6 B letter of application; formal style

7 *(Read the rubrics aloud and explain/elicit any unknown words. Allow Ss four to five mins. to complete the task. Ask individual Ss to report back to the class.)*

1 A letter of application
   B letter accepting an invitation
   C letter giving news
   D letter giving information
   E letter of complaint
   F letter congratulating someone

2 A the headmaster of the school
   B my friend
   C my friend
   D the person interested in learning French
   E the manager of the cereal company
   F my cousin

3   A   formal style
    B   informal style
    C   informal style
    D   formal style
    E   formal style
    F   informal style

4   **(Suggested answers)**
    A   Dear Sir, Yours faithfully + full name
    B   Dear + my friend's first name;
        Love + my first name
    C   Dear + my friend's first name;
        Take care + my first name
    D   Dear Mr/Ms/Mrs + person's surname, Yours sincerely + your full name
    E   Dear Sir/Madam, Yours faithfully + your full name
    F   Dear + my cousin's first name
        Love + my first name

5   **(Suggested answers)**
    A   Opening remarks: I am writing to apply for the position of teacher advertised in...
        Closing remarks: I would appreciate a reply at your earliest convenience.
    B   Opening remarks: Thanks a lot for the invitation, I'd love to come.
        Closing remarks: See you then!
    C   Opening remarks: You'll never guess where I've been.
        Closing remarks: Write back soon.
    D   Opening remarks: I am writing to give you the information you requested.
        Closing remarks: Do not hesitate to contact me...
    E   Opening remarks: I am writing to complain about...
        Closing remarks: I hope the matter will be resolved...
    F   Opening remarks: I have just heard the great news and would like to congratulate you.
        Closing remarks: Well done!

Unit 2 - Informal Letters (pp. 20 - 25)

1   *(Read the questions aloud and explain/elicit the meaning of any unknown words, then Ss do the listening task and answer the questions. Check Ss' answers, then ask individual Ss to talk about the letter.)*

1 B   2 A   3 A, B, E, F

2   *(Read out the theory and the paragraph plan. Explain/Elicit the meaning of any unknown terminology. Then ask Ss comprehension questions to make sure they have understood the theory. Read the rubric and the questions aloud. Help Ss to identify the key words in the rubric, then Ss complete the task. Check Ss' answers.)*

Key words: you recently moved to a big city — decided to write to a friend from your old neighbourhood — letter — describing life in your new city — feelings about the change

1   A friend of yours.
2   In my old neighbourhood.
3   In a big city.
4   To tell my friend about the city.
5   Topics: a) life in the big city
              b) feelings about the change
6   Dear + my friend's first name
    Lots of love/Best wishes + my first name
7   • constant noise from cars (negative)
    • ugly grey buildings (negative)
    • plenty of sports facilities (positive)
    • choice of things to do (positive)
    • huge crowds (negative)
    • good public transport system (positive)
    • large modern shops (positive)
8   **(Suggested answers)**
    Unfortunately, there is heavy traffic.
    I can't get used to the ugly grey buildings.
    I like living here because there are plenty of sports facilities.
    What I like most is that there is a wide choice of things to do.
    I hate huge crowds.
    The best thing is that there is a good public transport system.
    I like living here because there are large modern shops.
9   You can get around easily.
    You can make lots of new friends.
    You can do lots of different things.
    You can't walk home safely at night.
10 2 = c I feel pleased **as** there are always new things to do.
    3 = b I feel unsafe **because** there's more crime in the city.
    4 = e I feel disgusted **because** there's rubbish everywhere.
    5 = a I feel excited **because** the city never sleeps.

Unit 2

3 a) *(Allow Ss three or four mins. to read the letter and complete the task. Explain/Elicit the meaning of any words Ss do not understand. Then, check Ss' answers.)*

1 I've taken	5 had
2 I'd drop	6 didn't
3 haven't got	7 you've been
4 I'll never	8 heard

Para 2: life in the new city
Para 3: writer's feelings about the change
Para 4: closing remarks

b) Topic sentences in the letter:
Para 2: Birmingham is a really exciting city with millions of things to do.
Para 3: I like living here now, but I sometimes feel homesick as I miss lots of things about Gowrie.

(Suggested answers)
Para 2: Birmingham is a great city to live in.
Para 3: I enjoy living here but, there are some things I miss about my old city.

4 *(Explain/Elicit that the words in brackets introduce clauses of concession, then explain the meaning of any unknown words/phrases. Allow Ss three or four mins. to look at the pictures and complete the task. Check Ss' answers.)*

- There are lots of things to do. **However,** heavy traffic makes it difficult to get around.
- **Although** there are plenty of sports centres, they are expensive to join.
- There are few buses and trains. **Nevertheless,** they always arrive on time.
- **Although** there are no restaurants, there are a few inns that serve delicious homemade food.

5 *(Present the theory, then read sentences 1 - 8 aloud and help Ss to match them to points a - h in the theory box. As an extension, Ss can tell you examples of their own practising the theory presented.)*

3 g   4 h   5 e   6 d   7 f   8 c

6 *(Read out the theory table, then ask Ss to give examples of informal writing. Allow Ss three or four mins. to complete the task in Ex. 6. Check Ss' answers around the class asking Ss to justify their choice.)*

2 formal
3 informal (colloquial expression: *give ... a hug*)
4 informal (phrasal verb: *are you up*)
5 informal (short forms: *we're*)
6 formal
7 informal (short forms: *You'd never believe*, phrasal verb: *getting on*)

7 *(Read the extracts aloud and explain/elicit the meaning of any unknown words. Allow Ss about four mins. to complete the task, then check Ss' answers.)*

1 Sorry	6 that's all for now
2 ages	7 write soon
3 really	8 can't wait to hear
4 drop you a line	9 you've been up to
5 let you know	10 Lots of love

8 *(Ss work in pairs to complete the task. Ask individual pairs to report back to the class.)*

	Opening remarks	Closing remarks
2	Hello! How are you? I'm writing to invite you to my birthday party on 2nd July.	Please come. It'll be great fun.
3	I'm really sorry about not being able to come to your party.	Sorry again. Please write and tell me all your news.
4	The reason I'm writing is to ask you if you could advise me on how to lose weight.	Write back soon and tell me what you think I should do.

9 *(Allow Ss two or three mins. to complete the task. Then, check Ss' answers around the class.)*

2 Write and tell me ~~how~~ it's like in Paris. **what**
3 I still can't get used to ~~wake~~ up so early in the morning. **waking**
4 I thought I'd write and ask you to give me ~~an~~ advice. **some**
5 I hope that everything will turn ~~up~~ all right. **out**
6 Sorry I haven't written ~~from~~ ages but I've been busy. **for**
7 ~~Write~~ me a line and tell me all your news. **Drop**
8 I'm writing to apologise ~~about~~ not coming to your wedding. **for**
9 I look forward to ~~hear~~ from you soon. **hearing**
10 Don't you think my news ~~are~~ exciting? **is** (*news* is an uncountable noun)

Unit 2

10 *(Explain/Elicit the meaning of any unknown words. Then allow Ss three or four mins. to read the rubrics and complete the task. Check Ss' answers.)*

    B two main body paragraphs
       Para 2: describe your new house
       Para 3: invite your friend to spend a weekend with you

    C two main body paragraphs
       Para 2: thank your uncle for invitation
       Para 3: ask what to buy as a wedding present

    D three main body paragraphs
       Para 2: invite friend to join you
       Para 3: give details of places you'll visit
       Para 4: suggest what friend should take

    E three main body paragraphs
       Para 2: describe school
       Para 3: describe teachers and timetable
       Para 4: give details of extra activities the school offers

11 *(Allow Ss three or four mins. to complete the task, then check Ss' answers around the class.)*

(Suggested answers)
1 Would you like to come to dinner at my house next Monday?
2 Why don't we spend the weekend in the mountains?
3 What about going shopping in the city centre?
4 Perhaps we could visit an art gallery while we're in London.

12 *(Ss work in pairs to make similar dialogues as in the example. Ss, in pairs, report back to the class.)*

(Suggested answers)
2 A: How about meeting at the park in the afternoon?
   B: That sounds good. We could go for a walk.
3 A: What about meeting at the castle in the morning?
   B: That sounds good. We could buy some souvenirs.
4 A: Why don't we meet at Peter's Café at noon?
   B: Yes, OK. We could have lunch.
5 A: Would you like to meet at the Fairview Shopping Centre at 4:30 pm?
   B: Yes, why not? We could go shopping.
6 A: Why don't we meet at the Odeon Cinema at 8:00 pm?
   B: That's a good idea. We could see a film.

13 *(Read the rubric aloud, then allow Ss five or six mins. to complete the task. Check Ss' answers.)*

a) (Ss' own answers)

b) (Suggested answer)

    First of all, I thought that we might visit the castle. It's in the old town and, from the hill that it stands on, the view is breathtaking. Then, perhaps we could go shopping at Fairview Shopping Centre. You can buy some fantastic souvenirs there at excellent prices.
    Finally, I think we should definitely go to Peter's Café for dinner. The fresh fish there is absolutely delicious. You'll love it! After that, how about going dancing in one of the many exciting clubs in the town?

14 *(Read the rubric aloud and help Ss to identify the key words. Ss complete the task; check Ss' answers around the class.)*

a) Key words: go on holiday – summer – don't have enough money – letter to a friend – asking for advice – ways to earn extra money
1 To ask for advice.
2 A friend of mine.
3 One paragraph.
4 **(Suggested answer)**

   Do you think I should...?
   What do you think I should do? etc

b) • I was wondering if you had any ideas about ...
    • Can you think of anything that ...?
    • What would you advise me to ...?

15 *(Explain/Elicit the meaning of any unknown words, then allow Ss three or four mins. to complete the task. Check Ss' answers.)*

(Suggested answers)
2 = d You should join a club. That way you'll meet new people.
3 = a Have you thought about talking to your teacher? If you do this, you'll get extra help.
4 = e Why don't you get a part-time job? Then you'll earn some money.
5 = c If I were you, I'd apologise to him/her. If you do this, you'll be friends again.

Unit 3

16 *(Allow Ss two or three mins. to read the letter, and complete the task. Check Ss' answers.)*

   a) 2 E   3 C   4 F   5 B   6 D

   b) Pam advises her to get a Saturday job in a local shop or babysit for neighbours.
   (Suggested answers)
   Mary could also deliver morning newspapers.
   Opening remarks:
   I've just got your letter and I think I can offer some advice.
   Closing remarks:
   I hope that one of my suggestions brings results.

17 *(Read the rubric aloud, then allow Ss three or four mins. to underline the key words and answer the questions. Check Ss' answers around the class.)*

   Key words: pen friend — asking for advice — improve his/her eating habits and get fit — write letter offering advice

   1 To offer advice. A pen friend of yours.
   2 Two: a) eating habits
              b) how to get fit
   3 **(Suggested answer)**
   Opening remarks:
   I'm glad to hear that you want to improve your eating habits and get fit. I'll try to advise you as best as I can.
   Closing remarks:
   Well, I hope you find my advice helpful. Write back and let me know how you get on.

   4 2 c You should try not to eat so much junk food and sweets. If you do this, your body won't store so much sugar and fat.
      3 a I think the best thing would be to eat plenty of fish, fruit and vegetables. If you follow a balanced diet, you won't put on weight.
      4 b You shouldn't go everywhere by car or by bus. That way, your body won't become lazy.

18 *(Help Ss to complete the task orally. When satisfied that Ss can deal with the task successfully, assign it as written HW.)*

(Suggested answer)
Dear Rachel,
   I'm glad to hear that you want to improve your eating habits and get fit. I'll try to advise you as best as I can.
   First of all, if I were you, I would eat plenty of fish, fruit and vegetables. If you follow a balanced diet, you won't put on weight. What is more, the best thing for you would be to try not to eat so much junk food, sweets and so on. If you do this, your body won't store so much sugar and fat.
   Another good idea is to join a gym and exercise regularly. This will mean that you'll soon get in shape and feel fitter. Finally, you shouldn't go everywhere by car or by bus. That way, your body won't become lazy.
   Well, I hope you find my advice helpful. Write back and let me know how you get on.
Love,
Lynn

Unit 3 - Formal Letters (pp. 26 - 33)

1 a) *(Read the first question aloud and ensure Ss understand the task. Then, Ss listen and tick the correct boxes. Check Ss' answers.)*

   1 A Letter 3 ✓   C Letter 2 ✓
      B Letter 1 ✓

b) *(Read questions 2-4 aloud, and explain/elicit the meaning of any unknown words. Ss listen again and complete the task. Check Ss' answers.)*

   2 B Letters 2 and 3 ✓
      C Letter 1   ✓
   3 A Letter 1   ✓
      B Letter 3   ✓
      C Letter 2   ✓
      D Letter 3   ✓
      E Letter 2   ✓
      F Letter 1   ✓
   4 A Letters 2 and 3 ✓
      C Letter 1   ✓

(Go through the theory and the paragraph plan and explain the meaning of any unknown terminology. Ask comprehension questions to make sure Ss have understood the theory. Do the same to present the theory concerning letters of application.)

Unit 3

2 *(Read the rubric and advertisement and help Ss underline the key words. Then, Ss answer the questions.)*

Key words: advertisement — local newspaper — apply for the job — St George's Primary School — looking for young, energetic and experienced school teacher — must be good organiser — keen on sports — apply in writing — Mrs Hunter — giving details of qualifications, skills and previous experience — saying why — you are suitable for the job

1 Mrs Hunter.   6 B, C, E
2 No, I don't.   7 B, C, E
3 Formal style.   8 A
4 To apply for the job. 9 B, D
5 C

3 *(Allow Ss three mins. to do the task, then check Ss' answers.)*

Para 1: opening remarks/reason(s) for writing
Para 2: age/present job/qualifications
Para 3: experience
Para 4: personal qualities
Para 5: closing remarks

- **Qualifications:** BSc degree, certificate in Education
  Experience: has been working for Margate Education Department since 1999 - has taught a variety of subjects (e.g. English, General Science, Games)
  Personal Qualities: punctual, hard-working, fair, good organisational skills
- *(Ss' own answer)*

4 *(Allow Ss three mins. to find the corresponding expressions, then check Ss' answers.)*

- I am interested in applying for ...
- I completed my certificate in Education ...
- I have been working for ...
- I consider myself to be punctual ...
- I enjoy working with children ...
- I enclose a reference from my present employer.
- I would be grateful if you would consider my application.
- I am available for interview ...
- I look forward to hearing from you.

5 2 am attending   4 joined   6 awarded
      3 studied   5 am a member

6 *(Present the theory concerning formal style and explain the meaning of any unknown terminology/ vocabulary, then ask Ss comprehension questions to make sure they have understood the theory.)*

a) *(Allow Ss two or three mins. to skim the letters and label the paragraphs. Check Ss' answers.)*

Para 2: age/qualifications
Para 3: experience, personal qualities
Para 4: other information
Para 5: closing remarks

b) *(Allow Ss a further three or four mins. to read the letters again and underline the correct phrases. Check Ss' answers and elicit which style is more suitable. Explain/Elicit the meaning of any words which Ss do not understand. [Point out that Ss do not need to know every word and draw their attention to the most relevant vocabulary e.g. **position, edition, ambition, enthusiastic**, etc.] Finally, ask individual Ss to read aloud from the letters.)*

- Letter A has an appropriate greeting and ending.
- **Phrases to be underlined:** I am writing to apply for the position of part-time shop assistant which was advertised - I passed the examination for the First Certificate in English with grade A - It is my ambition to become - Despite my lack of formal work experience, I feel that I would be well-suited for the position - I was described by the librarian as enthusiastic, dedicated and reliable - I will have no other commitments - I may be contacted - I look forward to receiving a reply in due course.
- The style used in Letter A. A letter of application is always written in a formal style, which means that the letter should contain complex sentences, advanced vocabulary, no short forms etc.

c) Steffi Braun applied for job A.

7 *(Ss, in pairs complete the task. Check Ss' answers around the class asking Ss to justify their answers by giving examples from the two letters.)*

1 B   3 B   5 A   7 A   9 B
2 A   4 B   6 B   8 A   10 A

8 *(Read the rubric and questions aloud. Explain/Elicit the meaning of any unknown words. Help Ss to identify the key words, then Ss answer the questions. Check Ss' answers.)*

13

Unit 3

Key words: advertisement — local newspaper — apply for the job — young helpers (18-25) needed — summer camp for 10-14 year olds — must speak English or French — able to work any time — 5th — 25th July — apply to Ben Carroll.

1. A, C, E, F, H, I
2. Skills: B, F, G, H
   Qualifications: I
   Experience: C, D
   Personal qualities: A
3. No, I don't.
4. To apply for the job.
5. Dear Mr Carroll,
   Yours sincerely,
   my full name

9 *(Help individual Ss to complete the task orally using their answers from Ex. 8 and the model in Ex. 3. When satisfied that Ss can deal with the task successfully, assign it as written HW.)*

(Suggested answer)

Dear Mr Caroll,

I am writing to apply for the position of (camp) helper which was advertised in yesterday's edition of *The Hatfield Gazette*.

I am an 18-year-old student. I have been awarded certificates in both English and French and I speak both fluently.

I worked in a summer camp last year and I am good at organising outdoor activities and sports events. Therefore, I feel that I would be well-suited for the position. Also, I regard myself as energetic and sociable, I am a good organiser and I like working with children.

As the month of July falls in the summer holidays, I will be available to work at any time for as many hours as needed, including evenings.

I can be contacted for interview by telephone on 7682301. I look forward to hearing from you.
Yours sincerely,
Marc Singer

10 *(Ask Ss to think of various situations in which they would write a letter of complaint (e.g. to a fast food restaurant manager to complain about poor service.) Present the theory concerning letters of complaint and explain/elicit the meaning of any unknown words. Point out the use of a mild or strong tone in such letters.)*

(Read the rubric and the questions aloud. Explain/ Elicit the meaning of any unknown words, then Ss, in pairs, underline the key words and complete the task. Check Ss' answers.)

Key words: you bought a calculator — given wrong model by mistake — you complained — shop assistant rude — write letter — complaints department — explaining reasons for dissatisfaction — action you expect the company to take

1. A person at the company's complaints department.
2. No, I don't.
3. To make a complaint.
4. **(Suggested answer)**
   I would use a strong tone because I am extremely upset about the matter.
5. **(Suggested answer)**
   Opening remarks: I am writing to express my strong dissatisfaction at the disgraceful treatment I received from one of your shop assistants.
   Closing remarks: I insist on a full refund or I shall be forced to take the matter further.

11 a) *(Read the words/phrases aloud and check that Ss understand their meaning. Allow Ss four or five mins. to read the letter and complete the task.)*

1. Firstly
2. However
3. Furthermore
4. To make matters worse
5. not only
6. but also
7. in addition to

b) Para 1: opening remarks/reason(s) for writing
Para 2: 1st complaint & examples/reasons
Para 3: 2nd complaint & examples/reasons
Para 4: 3rd complaint & examples/reasons
Para 5: closing remarks

c) 1. Mrs Adams is complaining because of the disgraceful treatment she received when purchasing a calculator.
2. • She was given the wrong model.
   • The calculator was cheaper and more basic.
   • She was deeply offended by the behaviour of the sales assistant when she went to complain.
3. Yes, she does.
   • given the wrong model → agreed to buy model X-401 → but was given model X-201
   • calculator cheaper → had fewer features and was more basic

14

Unit 3

- offended by behaviour of sales assistant → was impolite and unhelpful and refused to contact the manager
4 • A full refund ✓
  • An apology ✓
5 She will be forced to take further action.
6 She has used a strong tone.
  (words/phrases to be underlined)
  my strong dissatisfaction — disgraceful treatment — deeply offended — extremely upset — must insist — forced to take further action

12 2 → E strong tone
    3 → E mild tone
    4 → B strong tone

13 1 B → Letter III
       C → Letter II

(Suggested answers)

1 Despite the fact that I have already paid, the equipment has still not been delivered and I urgently need it.
2 Contrary to what the advertisement stated, there was no swimming pool, the rooms were extremely small and there was no maid service.
3 The model I received was not the model advertised on television. It was a huge, ugly, old-fashioned model.

  2 A 3 → Letter I
     B 1 → Letter III
     C 2 → Letter II

14 **(Suggested answers)**
  a) The Headmaster of the school.
  b) the noise made by the children's portable radios is unbearable — they are constantly littering my garden with rubbish
  c) **Opening remarks:**
  I am writing to draw your attention to the problem caused by some students from your school.
  Closing remarks:
  I hope that this matter will be resolved promptly.

15 **(Suggested answers)**
  2 **In spite of the fact** that I paid for a set of five compact discs, there were only three in the box.
  3 The advertisement said the tent was waterproof, **but** rain continually dripped in.
  4 **Although** the bicycle was brand new, the chain came off the first time I rode it.

5 The battery went flat after only two hours. **However**, the instructions said the battery lasted for sixteen hours.

16 *(Read the rubric and the questions aloud and explain/elicit the meaning of any unknown words. Then, Ss in pairs, underline the key words and complete the task. Check Ss' answers.)*

Key words: went for a meal — Benny's fast food restaurant — service very slow — food badly cooked — complained — supervisor rude — insisted on your paying for meal — write letter of complaint — head office — explaining reasons — saying what you expect company to do

1 To complain about the service, the meal and the supervisor's rudeness.
2 No, I don't.
3 **(Suggested answer)**
  I would use a strong tone because I am extremely upset about what happened.
4 Dear Sir/Madam,

  Yours faithfully,
  my full name
5 Three main body paragraphs
  Para 2: service slow
  Para 3: meal badly cooked
  Para 4: supervisor very rude
6 *(Check that Ss understand the vocabulary and the situation presented. Elicit suitable sentences around the class.)*
  (Suggested answer)
  1 **Despite** the restaurant's claim of fast service, I had to wait fifteen minutes to give my order and a further twenty minutes for the food to be served.
  2 The advertisement claims that Benny's serves delicious food. **However**, the chips were raw, the meat was frozen in the middle and the tomatoes were rotten.
  3 The restaurant claims that their customers always come first. **Nevertheless**, when I complained, the supervisor insisted on my paying for the meal, and when I refused, he rudely told me to leave.
7 **(Suggested answer)**
  To give me a full refund and improve their service. I would write my demands in the final paragraph of my letter.

Unit 4

17 *(Explain/Elicit the meaning of any unknown words, then allow Ss three or four mins. to read the extracts and complete the task. Check Ss' answers, then ask Ss to read the corrected extracts aloud.)*

- Paragraph A is a closing remark and paragraph B is an opening remark.

A 1 As you can imagine
2 I am extremely upset
3 I feel I am entitled to
4 a full refund
5 a written apology
6 I look forward to receiving your prompt reply

B 1 I am writing to express
2 my complete dissatisfaction
3 I was served
4 my anger
5 the behaviour of the supervisor
6 complained

18 *(Help individual Ss to complete the letter orally using their answers to Exs. 16 and 17. When satisfied that Ss can deal with the task successfully, assign it as written HW.)*

(Suggested answer)

Dear Sir/Madam,
 I am writing to express my complete dissatisfaction with the meal I was served last night at the local branch of Benny's, and my anger at the behaviour of the supervisor when I complained.
 Firstly, the service was extremely slow. Despite the restaurant's claim of fast service, I had to wait fifteen minutes to give my order, and a further twenty minutes for the food to be served.
 Furthermore, the advertisement describes the food at Benny's as delicious. However, the chips were raw, the meat was still frozen in the middle and the tomatoes were rotten.
 To make matters worse, even though the restaurant claims that their customers always come first, when I complained the supervisor insisted on my paying for the meal, and when I refused he rudely told me to leave.
 As you can imagine, I am extremely upset. I feel I am entitled to a full refund, in addition to a written apology from the local manager. I look forward to receiving your prompt reply.

Yours faithfully,
Maria Sanchez

Unit 4 - Semi-formal Letters (pp. 34 - 37)

1 *(Read the questions aloud and explain/elicit the meaning of any unknown words. Then, Ss do the listening task. Check Ss' answers.)*

1 B   2 C   3 C, E

2 *(Present the theory and the paragraph plan, then read the rubric, extracts and questions aloud. Explain/Elicit the meaning of any unknown vocabulary and help Ss to identify the key words in the rubric. Ss complete the task. Check Ss' answers.)*

Key words: You are going – language school in Britain – stay with Mr and Mrs Jackson – Jacksons ask for information – write a letter - giving information asked for – including questions or requests of your own

1 Mr and Mrs Jackson
2 To give information, ask questions and make requests
3 Three main body paragraphs
4 a, b, d
5 **(Suggested answers)**

 a) As far as food is concerned, I have no special requests.
 b) The only thing I don't eat is chicken soup.
 c) My favourite food is spaghetti Bolognese.
 d) I am looking forward to trying shepherd's pie.

6 **(Suggested answers)**

 a) I was wondering if it is necessary for me to bring a thick jumper.
 b) Perhaps you could tell me if it gets cold in the evenings.
 c) I would like to know if the town has a post office.
 d) What is the public transport like? Is it reliable/ frequent?
 e) Do you think I need to bring a swimming costume?

7 **(Suggested answers)**

 Opening remarks:
 I would like to thank you for your letter.
 Closing remarks:
 It was very kind of you to write. I'm looking forward to meeting you.

3 *(Allow Ss three or four mins. to skim the letter and complete the task. Check Ss' answers.)*

Unit 4

1 Thank you very much
2 I am writing
3 I need to
4 It is very kind
5 As far as food is concerned
6 Besides
7 I was wondering if you had
8 Best wishes

Para 1: opening remarks/reason(s) for writing
Para 2: travel plans
Para 3: food requirements
Para 4: further questions
Para 5: closing remarks

4 *(Present the theory, paying special attention to the examples. Explain/Elicit the meaning of any unknown vocabulary. Allow Ss two or three mins. to read the extracts and complete the task. Check Ss' answers by asking individual Ss to read the corrected extracts aloud.)*

1 Mrs Ames
2 Thank you for the invitation
3 received
4 I apologise for
5 reply
6 I will be unable to visit
7 don't hesitate
8 telephone me
9 any help
10 the preparations
11 a great success
12 Best wishes

5 *(Allow Ss two mins. to complete the task. Check Ss' answers.)*

2 F   3 A   4 E   5 B   6 D

6 a) *(Ensure Ss understand the task, then elicit suitable answers from the class.)*

1 formal   2 informal   3 semi-formal

b) *(Allow Ss about two mins. to complete the task. Check Ss' answers, asking them to justify their answers.)*

A 1   B 2   C 3

7 a) *(Read the rubric and the questions aloud. Then, allow Ss two or three mins. to underline the key words and answer the questions. Check Ss' answers.)*

Key words: just returned from Britain — school had arranged for you to stay with a local couple you had not met before — write a letter - thanking them for their kindness.

1 The local couple whom I stayed with. Not very well.
2 Semi-formal style. I will use a polite tone. I won't use much colloquial language, idioms, phrasal verbs or short forms.
3 To thank them for their kindness to me during my stay.
4 C

b) *(Allow Ss four mins. to complete the task. Check Ss' answers by asking individual Ss to read their sentences aloud and say which topic sentence each is related to.)*

A My room was very comfortable and every meal was delicious.(Para 2)
B What helped me most was the chance to practise English with you every day. (Para 3)
C You made me feel like I was part of the family.(Para 2)
D I never thought (that) I would be able to speak English so well. (Para 3)

c) *(Allow Ss two or three mins. to read the extract and the phrases and complete the task. Explain/ Elicit the meaning of any unknown words. Check Ss' answers by asking individual Ss to read the completed extract aloud.)*

2 B   3 B   4 A

d) *(Read items A-H aloud, then elicit the correct answers from Ss.)*

C ✓   F ✓   G ✓

8 *(Help Ss to compose their letter orally, using their answers from Ex. 7. When satisfied that Ss can deal with the task successfully, assign it as written HW.)*

(Suggested answer)

Dear Mr and Mrs Jackson,
 I am writing to tell you that I have arrived home safely, and to thank you both very much for being so kind to me during my stay with you. It was a wonderful experience which I am sure I will always remember.
 I really appreciate all your efforts that made my stay in your home a happy one. My room was very comfortable and every meal was delicious. You made me feel like I was part of the family.
 My trip to Britain has certainly improved my English, too. What helped me most was the chance to practise English with you every day. I never thought (that) I would be able to speak English so well.

Thank you again for all your kindness. My parents send their regards and ask me to tell you that you will always be welcome guests if you would like to visit my country. I would love to hear from you whenever you have time to write.
Best wishes,
Julia Buitoni

Unit 5 - Transactional Letters (pp. 38 - 41)

1 *(Read the advertisement and the notes aloud. Explain/Elicit the meaning of any unknown words, then Ss listen and complete the task. Check Ss' answers.)*

A ✓ advert in Wessex Times, April
C ✓ bikes — hire, or bring my own?
E ✓ hiking — where? — with a guide?
F ✓ any other activities offered?
G ✓ total cost — how much?
H ✓ charge per day, or per activity?
J ✓ necessary to book?
K ✓ write, or phone me — 0181-313-9480

2 *(Present the theory and explain/elicit the meaning of any unknown vocabulary. Then read the rubric and the advertisement aloud. Help Ss to identify the key words in the rubric, pointing out that all the notes are essential. Then elicit answers to the questions.)*

Key words: you and two friends decided to rent the cottage — read advertisement and notes — write letter to fourth friend — asking him/her to join you — giving him/her the information about cottage — what you can do there

1 A friend of mine
2 Yes, I am, because it's an informal letter to a friend.
3 To ask a friend to join me and two other friends on holiday.
4 B
5 ✓ A
  ✓ C
  ✓ E
  ✓ G
  ✓ H
  ✓ J

6 2 A   3 B   4 A
7 **(Suggested answers)**
Opening remarks
Hi! How are you? I'm writing to invite you to join us this August in Dorset.
Closing remarks
Well, I must go now. Please write back and let me know if you're interested in joining us.

3 a) *(Allow Ss four or five mins. to read the letter, complete the paragraph plan and underline the correct words/phrases. Explain/Elicit the meaning of any unknown words, then check Ss' answers.)*

Para 2: information about the cottage
Para 3: what the area offers
Para 4: persuade friend to join you

Yes, all the points in the rubric, advertisement and notes have been covered in the letter.

words/phrases to be underlined: cottage in Dorset, 15th to 21st August, love it if you can join us, two bedrooms, big, two beds in each, large garden, £200 a week, £50 each, lots of things to do in area, horse riding, sports centre not far away, market, local museum, wildlife park, four bikes

b) (Suggested answers)
- The owner's description of the house sounds fantastic.
- You can't imagine what we can do there.
- We would be really happy if you choose to come with us.

4 *(Present the theory, then allow Ss four or five mins. to complete the task. Check Ss' answers around the class.)*

(Suggested answers)

3 I = How many tickets are available?
4 I = Are there any facilities for young children?
5 D = Could you perhaps inform me what time the play finishes?
6 D = I would like to know if/whether you cater for vegetarians.
7 I = Could you send me further information?
8 D = I would be grateful if you could tell me where exactly the restaurant is.
9 I = Where is the nearest train station?
10 D = I would like to know if/whether the cost of equipment is included in the price.

Unit 6

5 *(Explain/Elicit the meaning of any unknown vocabulary, then allow Ss three or four mins. to complete the task. Check Ss' answers.)*

b	4	e	7	h	10
c	3	f	5	i	6
d	2	g	9	j	8

6 a) *(Read the advertisement aloud and explain/elicit the meaning of any unknown vocabulary. Allow Ss four or five mins. to complete the task. Check Ss' answers.)*

(Suggested answers)

2 How old? 4 Private room?
3 Which evenings? 5 What exactly? A car?

b) (Suggested answers)

2 I would like to know how old candidates should be./Could you please tell me what age candidates should be?
3 I would like to know which evenings in particular are free./Could you please tell me which evenings are free?
4 I would like to know if you provide a private room./Could you please tell me whether you provide a private room?
5 I would like to know what exactly the benefits are and whether they include the use of a car./Could you please tell me what exactly the benefits are and whether they include the use of a car?

7 a) *(Read the rubric and the notes aloud. Explain/Elicit the meaning of any unknown vocabulary, then Ss complete the task. Check Ss' answers.)*

1 c
2 Mrs White
3 Not very well
4 Dear Mrs White, Yours sincerely, my full name
5 **(Suggested answer)**
Opening remarks
I'm writing with regard to the end-of-term party that I am organising.
Closing remarks
Thank you in advance. I look forward to hearing from you.

b) *(Allow Ss four or five mins. to read the notes again. Check Ss' answers by asking individual Ss to read the sentences aloud.)*

(Suggested answers)
- **who's coming:** The 4th and 5th forms will be attending the party.
- **music:** The music will be provided by *John Smith's Disco*.
- **food and drink:** Mary and Eva will be responsible for supplying the food and drink for the party.
- **cost of tickets:** How much should we charge for a ticket?
- **posters:** Where exactly can we put up the posters?

8 *(Help Ss to compose their letter orally using their answers from Ex. 7. When satisfied that Ss can deal with the task successfully, assign it as written HW.)*

(Suggested answer)
Dear Mrs White,
I'm writing with regard to the end-of-term party that I am organising.
Firstly, the party will be held in the school hall on Saturday 1st July from 8 pm to 11 pm. The 4th and 5th forms will be attending. The music will be provided by John Smith's Disco and Mary and Eva will be responsible for supplying the food and drink for the party.
Finally, I was wondering if you could advise me on how much we should charge for a ticket. Also, could you let me know where exactly we can put up the posters?
Thank you in advance. I look forward to hearing from you.
Yours sincerely,
Ben Adams

Unit 6 - Describing People (pp. 42 - 47)

1 *(Elicit from Ss words/phrases required to describe a person i.e. tall, short, thin, slim, blue eyes etc. Ask Ss to suggest as many words as they can. Explain that they are going to listen to someone describing his schoolfriends and that Ss should listen a) to identify the friends and b) for the words which describe their personalities. Then, Ss do the listening activity. Check Ss' answers. Finally, ask Ss to describe each boy.)*

a) 1 Martin 2 Alex 3 Ravi

b) 1 A   3 A   5 M
     2 M   4 R   6 R

Unit 6

(Suggested answer)

Martin is fairly tall and has short brown hair. He's really well-behaved and clever.
Alex is short with red hair and rosy cheeks. He's really funny, but he's sometimes a bit naughty.
Ravi is quite tall and slim with dark hair. He's a bit quiet, but he's very sporty.

2 *(Present the theory and the paragraph plan and elicit the main topic of each paragraph. Read the rubric aloud and explain/elicit the meaning of any unknown words. Elicit the key words to be underlined. Then, read the questions aloud and allow Ss four mins. to complete the task. Check Ss' answers)*

Key words: editor - school magazine - article about a close friend - describing - appearance - personality - hobbies/interests

1   passive voice ✗   linking words ✔
    colloquial language ✔ complex sentences ✗
    abbreviations ✔
2   B
3   A, B and D because they are not close friends.
4   paragraph 1
5   paragraph 5
6   B, E and F

3 a) *(Explain/Elicit the meaning of any unknown vocabulary. Allow Ss three or four mins. to complete the task, then elicit answers from individual Ss around the class. Write the completed table on the board. Ss copy the completed table into their notebooks, then make sentences using the words/phrases.)*

	Topic	Main Points
MAIN BODY Para 2	appearance	good-looking, great sense of style, olive skin, curly dark hair, casual clothes, wavy hair, pale complexion, pointed nose, shoulder-length hair, tall, slim, of medium height, attractive, plump
Para 3	personal qualities	fantastic sense of humour, immature, outgoing, friendly, rude, lazy, generous, popular, bossy
Para 4	hobbies/ interests	sailing, painting, scuba diving, skiing, rafting

(Ss' own answers)

b) *(Allow Ss two or three mins. to skim the text and label the paragraphs. Check Ss' answers. Ss underline the topic sentences, then in pairs think of other appropriate ones. Ask some Ss to report back to the class.)*

Para 2: physical appearance/clothes
Para 3: personal qualities
Para 4: hobbies/interests
Para 5: comments/feelings

(Suggested answers)

Para 1: I first met Jaqcues, my best friend, two years ago.
Para 2: Jacques is a very handsome man.
Para 3: Jacques has got an outgoing personality.
Para 4: Jacques likes sports a lot, especially water sports.
Para 5: I'm really lucky to have a great friend like Jacques.

4 *(Present the theory, then allow Ss three or four mins. to read the text again. Explain/Elicit the meaning of any unknown words. Ss complete the task. Check Ss' answers.)*

Adjectives to be circled: quite good-looking, tall, slim, olive skin, curly dark hair, great sense of style, well-dressed, casual clothes, very outgoing, friendly, loves to have fun, fantastic sense of humour, a bit immature
Yes, he does: Jacques can be a bit immature at times.
Yes, the writer does: When Jacques doesn't get what he wants, he acts childishly and stamps his feet.

5 *(Present the theory on linking words, then allow Ss two or three mins. to fill in the correct words. Check Ss' answers.)*

1   with, but, and   3   both, also, as well as
2   who, with, and   4   and, also, However

*(In preparation for Ex. 6, write a table on the board with the headings **height, build, age, face, complexion, hair, eyes, nose, special features** and **dress style**. Elicit from Ss as many descriptive words as possible and write them in the appropriate column in the table. Ss copy the table into their notebooks as a reference for the following exercise.)*

20

(Suggested answers)

height	short, tall, of medium height, of average height etc.
build	heavy build, of medium build etc.
age	young, middle-aged, old, elderly, in his early/mid/late thirties etc.
face	long, round etc.
complexion	pale, dark, fair etc.
hair	short, long, straight, curly, wavy, red, brown, shoulder-length etc.
eyes	blue, green, etc, big, small, almond-shaped
nose	pointed, small, big etc.
special features	dimples, scar, bruise, beard, moustache, freckles etc.
dress style	casually dressed, sportswear, business clothes

6 a) *(Ss, in pairs, choose the best answers, then add any new words from the exercise to the table.)*

2 a) medium
   b) middle-aged
   c) moustache

3 a) tall
   b) glasses
   c) business clothes

4 a) early teens
   b) curly hair
   c) dark complexion

5 a) long
   b) pale
   c) friendly

b) *(Read the example aloud. Ss describe each person.)*

(Suggested answers)

2 ... Mr Roberts is a man of medium build who is middle-aged and has a moustache.
3 Gerald is a tall man with glasses who wears business clothes.
4 Veronica is in her early teens with curly hair and a dark complexion.
5 Julie has got long hair, pale skin and a friendly expression.

7 *(Remind Ss that to describe a person you need to describe the person's character using various adjectives. Read the list of adjectives, then allow Ss three or four mins. to match the items. Help individual Ss to form sentences. The task can then be assigned as written HW.)*

b 10   d 11   f 4   h 12   j 7   l 8
c 5   e 6   g 3   i 2   k 9

(Suggested answers)

... My sister is a popular person who everyone likes. She can be rather impatient, however, because she hates waiting for anything.
My best friend is always well-dressed and wears smart clothes. She is also an energetic person who is very active.
My brother is an intelligent person who does well at school. He is also very cheerful and is always smiling.
My niece is rather bossy, and always tells everyone what to do.
My friend Mary, is very talkative, and is always chatting. However, she can be lazy because she doesn't like working hard.
My cousin can be a bit rude because he isn't polite to strangers. He is also selfish and cares only about himself.

8 *(Explain that items 1 to 8 refer to people's mannerisms. Allow Ss two or three mins. to complete the task, then elicit answers from individual Ss around the class. As an extension, Ss can think of other examples to justify the same character qualities.)*

1 generous   4 energetic   7 selfish
2 aggressive 5 cheerful   8 moody
3 impatient   6 lazy

9 *(Allow Ss two or three mins. to cross out the unnecessary words. Check Ss' answers, then explain/elicit the meanings of any unknown words. Finally, elicit suitable answers to the questions.)*

2 to   3 will   4 the   5 the   6 much

The first para is about Megan's personal qualities.
The second para is about Megan's hobby.
By giving examples of her mannerisms.
She blushes and then looks down at the floor.

10 *(Present the example, then read the topic sentences aloud and explain/elicit the meaning of any unknown words. Elicit suitable points for inclusion in each description, then in pairs Ss complete the task. Check Ss' answers around the class.)*

(Suggested answers)

1 He is tall and well-built, with dark hair and green eyes, as well as a cheerful, friendly expression.
2 He is often noisy and he loves running around the house, even when he has been told not to.
3 She is the best student in our class, and she always gets full marks in tests and exams.
4 Whenever I see her, she is well-dressed. She also spends a lot of time keeping fit and staying slim.
5 For example, he often goes mountain climbing and hang-gliding. He likes ballooning, too. He's also making plans to try bungee jumping.

11 *(Read the rubric aloud and elicit from Ss the key words to be underlined. Allow Ss another three or four mins. to read the text and complete the task.)*

a) **Key words:** teacher – composition – person who once helped you – describing – appearance – personal qualities – mannerisms – hobbies/interests

   A 4   B 1   C 5   D 3   E 2

b) Yes, all the points in the rubric have been included.

c) Past tenses, because the writer no longer sees the person.

d) linking words/phrases to be underlined:
   but – and – not only..., but also... (Para B1)
   and – with – which (Para E2)
   but – as well as – which – because – also – although – and (Para D3)
   and – and – also (Para A4)
   and – but – and – who (Para C5)

e) talked in a low voice, blushed easily

f) Topic sentences to be underlined and replaced: E - Ruth was pretty. = 3, Ruth was quite attractive.
   D - Ruth had a quiet but very friendly nature. = 2, Ruth was a gentle and affectionate person.
   A - In her spare time, Ruth liked to read. = 1, Ruth's favourite pastime was reading.

12 *(Read the rubric aloud and elicit the key words to be underlined, then Ss answer the questions.)*

Key words: local newspaper – description – work colleague or fellow student – admire – appearance – personal qualities/mannerisms – hobbies/interests

a) ii) a relative

b) semi-formal

c) present tenses, because you see this person often

d) *(Ss choose the appropriate points from the list.)*

   • his/her hobbies/interests
   • description of his/her appearance
   • name, when/where/how met
   • your comments/feelings
   • description of his/her personality/mannerisms

(Write the following headings on the board. Ss copy them into their notebooks, then fill in the appropriate information about the person they will describe. Individual Ss describe their colleague or fellow student using their notes.)

(Suggested answers)

Para 2: **height:** tall
        age: 27
        face: round
        hair: long, brown
        eyes: brown
        nose: small
        special features: dimples
        dress style: casual clothes, jeans/T-shirts
Para 3: **personality:** popular - everyone likes - impatient - hates waiting
Para 4: **hobbies/interests:** swimming - 3 times a week - listening to music - buys new CDs
Para 5: **your comments/feelings:** enjoy being with - always have fun - hope be friends for ever

13 (When satisfied that Ss can deal with the task successfully, assign it as written HW.)

(Suggested answer)

Julia is a colleague who I first met two years ago while we were having a lunch break in the canteen.

She is a tall slim 27-year-old. She has got long brown hair with a round face and brown eyes. She usually dresses casually in jeans and T-shirts.

Julia is a popular person who is liked by everyone. However, she is rather impatient at times and hates waiting for anything.

In her free time, Julia enjoys swimming and goes three times a week after work. She also likes listening to music and is always buying new CDs to listen to.

Julia is one of my best friends, and I enjoy being with her. We always have fun together, and I hope we will be friends forever.

Unit 7 - Describing Places/Buildings (pp. 48 - 53)

1 (Read the table aloud and explain/elicit the meanings of any unknown words. Ss do the listening task. Check Ss' answers around the class, then ask individual Ss to describe the city.)

Name:	Brussels	☐	Buenos Aires	✓	Bonn	☐
Location:	Argentina	✓	Africa	☐	Antarctica	☐
	centre of the country	☐	south-east coast	☐	north-east coast	✓
Things to see and do:	Plaza de Mayo	✓	National Gallery	☐	History Museum	☐
	Cathedral	✓	Spanish Tower	☐	Casa Rosada	✓
Shopping:	antiques fair	✓	big market	✓	superstore	☐
Nightlife:	dance halls	☐	cinemas	✓	variety of restaurants	✓
Comments:	better in August	☐	recommend it	✓	too noisy	☐

(Ss' own answers)

2 (Present the theory and the paragraph plan. Then, read the rubric and the questions aloud and explain/elicit the meaning of any unknown words. Allow Ss two or three mins. to underline the key words and answer the questions. Check Ss' answers.)

Key words: international travel magazine — town visited — article — describing a town — things to see and do — shops — nightlife

1 A descriptive article.
   The magazine's readers.
   No, because an article for an international travel magazine should be written in semi-formal style.

2 A, C, D, F

3 (Present the phrases of location. Individual Ss around the class talk about the location of the towns/cities on the map.)

(Suggested answers)
London is situated in the south-east of England.
Ipswich is located on the east coast of England.
Nottingham is located in the centre of England.
York is situated in the north-east of England.
Exeter is located in south-west England.

(As an extension, Ss talk about the location of towns/cities in their country.)

4 **a)** (Explain/Elicit the meaning of any unknown words. Then, allow Ss two or three mins. to say which words/phrases belong under each heading. Check Ss' answers.)

Things to see and do: museum, ancient theatre, zoo, café, temple, art gallery, botanical gardens, monument, statue, palace, funfair, amusement arcade
Shopping: boutique, open-air market, bazaar, fair, souvenir shop, antique shop, shopping centre
Nightlife: nightclub, restaurant, music hall, multi-screen cinema, theatre

Unit 7

b) *(Read the phrases and the examples aloud. Ss, in pairs, use the prompts to talk about their town. Ask some Ss to report back to the class.)*

(Ss' own answers)

5 a) *(Check that Ss understand the headings, then allow Ss two or three mins. to skim the article and label the paragraphs. Check Ss' answers. Finally, ask individual Ss to talk about Brighton.)*

Para 1: name, location, reason for choosing it
Para 2: things to see and do
Para 3: shopping
Para 4: nightlife
Para 5: comments/recommendation

b) *(Elicit what a topic sentence is, i.e. the first sentence in each paragraph which introduces or summarises the main topic of the paragraph. Allow Ss three or four mins. to underline the topic sentences and think of suitable alternatives. Check Ss' answers around the class.)*

(Suggested answers)

Para 2: There are lots of things to see and do in Brighton.
Para 3: Brighton offers plenty of choice if you like shopping.
Para 4: Nightlife in Brighton will not disappoint visitors.

c) *(Allow Ss two or three mins. to match the adjectives to their opposites. Check Ss' answers, then ask individual Ss to make sentences using the opposites.)*

charming → unattractive
peaceful → hectic
beautiful → ugly
famous → unknown
modern → old-fashioned
narrow → wide
exciting → boring
popular → unpopular
international → local

(Ss' own answers)

6 a) *(Present the theory, then ask Ss to look at the pictures and identify the places: A: seaside village, B: busy town, C: countryside. Ss match sentences 1 to 3 to pictures A to C. Check Ss' answers, then Ss identify the senses used. As an extension, Ss can make sentences about each picture using the senses.)*

1 C (hearing)   2 A (smell)   3 C (sight)

b) *(Ask Ss to look at picture B and think of words/ phrases related to the picture e.g. busy streets, rush hour, lots of people, crowded shops etc. Ss, then, in pairs make sentences using these phrases. Check Ss' answers.)*

(Suggested answers)

You can feel the energy of the city as you walk along the noisy main streets.
The city comes alive with the sound of traffic during the rush hour.

7 *(Present the theory on linking structures, then allow Ss two or three mins. to complete the task. Check Ss' answers.)*

1 Sydney is a large and interesting city **which** offers visitors a wide variety of sights to see and things to do.
2 It is full of exotic restaurants **where** you can enjoy a meal.
3 **Located** on the south-east cost of Australia, Sydney has one of the busiest harbours in the country.
4 **With** its wonderful blend of cultures and friendly people, Sydney is an ideal place for a holiday.

8 *(Explain these words: **cable car ride, species, samba halls**, then Ss complete the task. Check Ss' answers while individual Ss read aloud from the text.)*

a) 1 south   3 tropical   5 live
    2 famous   4 delicious   6 friendly

b) *(Help individual Ss to identify the key words in the rubric. Allow Ss two or three mins. to re-read the brochure in part a). Check Ss' answers around the class. Then, ask individual Ss to talk about Rio de Janeiro.)*

Key words: international travel magazine descriptions – places worth visiting – article – things to see and do – nightlife

1 No, because a magazine article should be written in semi-formal style.
2 Present tenses + past tenses for historical facts.
3 Points to be included in the main body paragraphs:
Para 2 (things to see and do): cable car ride up Sugar Loaf Mountain; take train up the Corvocado to the statue Cristo Redentor; the Botanical Gardens
Para 3 (nightlife): have dinner at a traditional restaurant – try "feijoada"; go to a musical or live show; dance at one of Rio's samba halls
4 the scent of fresh flowers → smell
the blazing heat of the sun → touch
people talking → hearing
spicy food → taste
the aroma of fresh coffee → smell
clear blue sky → sight
cold stone floors → touch
snow-covered mountains → sight

(Ss' own answers)

c) *(When satisfied that Ss can cope with the task orally, assign it as written HW.)*

(Suggested answer)

Rio de Janeiro is on the south-east coast of Brazil. It is a wonderful place for a holiday because it has lots of things to offer people of all ages.

There are lots of things to see and do in Rio. For example, no visit there is complete without a cable car ride up Sugar Loaf Mountain. Or why not take the train up the Corvocado to see the statue *Cristo Redentor*? It's a sight you shouldn't miss. Another option is the Botanical Gardens where you can smell the beautiful fresh flowers among almost 5000 species of tropical plants.

After a long day of sightseeing in the blazing heat of the sun, relax and have fun long into the night. Why not start with a dinner of spicy Brazilian food at a traditional restaurant? Try "feijoada" – it's delicious. Then, go on to see a musical or a live show. You can even learn to dance the Brazilian way at one of Rio's many samba halls.

Rio has something to offer everyone and the people are really friendly. I would recommend it for anyone who wants a holiday in an exotic place to get away from the stress of everyday life.

9 a) *(Read the table aloud and explain/elicit the meanings of any unknown words. Ss do the listening task. Check Ss' answers, then individual Ss talk about Buckingham Palace.)*

Name:	Buckingham Palace	✓	Windsor Castle	
Location:	outside London		in central London	✓
Historical Facts:	built in the 18th century	✓	built in the 8th century	
	official home since 1850	✓	official home since 1520	
Exterior:	made of marble small windows huge balcony garden with pool	✓ ✓	made of iron large windows narrow balcony garden with lake	✓ ✓
Interior:	100 rooms red carpets priceless photographs	✓	600 rooms red ceilings priceless paintings	✓ ✓
Comment:	not to be missed	✓	not worth long queues	

b) *(Explain the task, then allow Ss four or five mins. to write suitable sentences. Check Ss' answers around the class. Point out that Ss should use past tenses when they give the historical facts of the place.)*

(Suggested answers)

1 It was built in the 18th century, but has only been the Royal Family's official home since 1850.
2 It is made of marble, with large windows and a huge balcony at the front. At the back there is a garden with a small lake.
3 There are 600 rooms, with lots of red carpets and priceless paintings.

10 a) *(Present the theory on describing buildings. Then read the rubric and the questions. Elicit the key words to be underlined. Allow Ss two or three mins. to complete the task. Check Ss' answers.)*

Key words: reporter international travel magazine – articles about castles – article – describing famous castle – history – exterior – interior

Unit 7

1 Readers of the magazine.
2 **(Suggested answer)**
- tall towers
- thick stone walls
- small windows
- stone floors
- wooden furniture

b) *(Allow Ss five mins. to read the text and put the verbs into the correct tense. Help Ss to identify the active and passive verbs. Check Ss' answers around the class, then ask individual Ss to read aloud from the text.)*

1 is situated – passive
2 was built – passive
3 lived – active
4 made – active
5 is furnished – passive
6 was not designed – passive

c) *(Allow Ss three or four mins. to read the text again and complete the table. Check Ss' answers by asking individual Ss to describe the castle.)*

Historical Facts: built in 1212 – where the famous Prince Vlad Tepes once lived – inspiration for Bram Stoker's *Dracula*

Exterior: tall towers – thick stone walls – small windows

Interior: dark and gloomy – each room has a huge fireplace – furnished with simple wooden items – no paintings on walls – no carpets on cold stone floors

11 a) Exterior: red brick walls, well-kept garden, tall chimneys, little pond, large windows, flower beds full of beautiful flowers

Interior: tiled floor, colourful rug, staircase, bookshelves, wooden coffee table, leather sofas, unusual lamps, modern paintings

b) (Suggested answers)
- The furnishing includes a colourful rug, leather sofas and a wooden coffee table. There are some unusual lamps and modern paintings on the wall. There is also a staircase that leads up to the first floor.
- The building is very attractive, with red brick walls, tall chimneys and large windows. It also has a little pond and a well-kept garden with flower beds full of beautiful flowers.

12 a) *(Ask Ss to quickly skim the text and match each extract to the appropriate sources, then explain/ elicit the meaning of any unknown words.)*

A – an article in a travel magazine
B – an estate agent's advertisement
C – a story

b) 2 C   3 A

c) *(Allow Ss three or four mins. to complete the task. Check Ss' answers around the class.)*

(Suggested answer)

... Guess where we went on the last day of our holiday! We visited the Leaning Tower of Pisa. It is a tall, eight-storey tower which is made of coloured marble. It's an amazing sight.

13 a) *(Read the rubric aloud and elicit the key words to be underlined. Discuss the answers to questions 1 and 2 with the class. Then allow Ss about ten mins. to prepare their answers to the remaining questions. Check Ss' answers around the class, then ask individual Ss to talk about the building they have chosen.)*

Key words: teacher – description of most famous building in town – school magazine – historical facts – describing exterior and interior

1 My teacher.
   No, because a magazine article should be written in semi-formal style.
2 Five paragraphs.
   Para 1: name, location of building, reason for choosing it
   Para 2: historical facts
   Para 3: exterior
   Para 4: interior
   Para 5: comments/feelings, recommendation

3-9 *(Ss' own answers. Choose one specific building in Ss' town, then Ss, in pairs, answer questions 3 to 9. Write the headings in the table below on the board. While Ss answer questions 3-9, complete the table on the board. Ss copy completed table into their notebooks, then individual Ss describe the building.)*

Unit 8

(Suggested table)

Building location:	Winter Palace, St. Petersburg – by Neva River in Russia
Historical facts:	built 1754-1762 – main residence of the Russian Tsars – destroyed by fire (1837) – now fully restored
Exterior:	3 storeys high-built around a large square-exterior painted green & white- windows decorated with gold
Interior:	high marble arches – marble floors – rooms brightly lit and decorated with statues of Greek gods and famous paintings
Comments:	magnificent building – recommend to take a full day to explore it

b) *(When satisfied that Ss can deal with the task successfully, assign it as written HW.)*

(Suggested answer)

One of the major attractions of St. Petersburg is the Winter Palace. The Palace is located on the bank of the Neva River in Russia.

It was built between 1754 and 1762 and was the main residence of the Russian Tsars. Most of the original palace was destroyed by a fire in 1837, but it has now been fully restored.

The palace is three storeys high and is built around a large square. The exterior is painted green and white and the windows are decorated with gold.

The inside of the palace is stunning. There are high marble arches and marble floors. The rooms are brightly lit and richly decorated with statues of Greek gods in every corner and famous paintings on the walls.

All in all, the Winter Palace is a truly magnificent building. Visitors wishing to enjoy its many fabulous treasures are recommended to take a full day to explore it.

(Note: The sentences in bold are topic sentences. The rest of each paragraph is supporting sentences.)

Unit 8 - Describing Objects (pp. 54 - 55)

1 *(Ask Ss to look at pictures 1-3, and check that they understand the meanings of **suitcase, rucksack, nylon, plastic, leather, stickers**. Play the cassette [twice, if necessary]. Ss listen and complete the task. Check Ss' answers, elicit which object is referred to in the dialogue, then ask individual Ss to describe the object.)*

1	Place lost:	at the airport ☐	on the underground ✓	at the bus stop ☐
2	Time:	11:30 am ☐	11:30 pm ✓	1:30 pm ☐
3	Date:	5th December ☐	5th November ✓	6th September ☐
4	Item:	suitcase ✓	briefcase ☐	rucksack ☐
5	Size:	small ☐	medium ☐	large ✓
6	Colour:	light brown ☐	dark brown ☐	grey ✓
7	Material:	nylon ☐	plastic ✓	leather ☐
8	Special features:	shoulder strap ☐	wheels ☐	stickers ✓

- Picture A shows the object referred to in the dialogue.

(Suggested answer)

- It is a large grey suitcase. It is made of plastic and has a lot of brightly-coloured stickers on it.

27

Unit 8

(Present the theory box and explain/elicit the meanings of any unknown words. As an optional extension, give a number of adjectives as examples, and ask Ss to identify whether each is an opinion adjective or a fact adjective. Ss may also be asked to describe objects in the classroom. Allow Ss two or three mins. to complete the task. Check Ss' answers, then explain/elicit the meanings of any unknown words.)

2 a) 1 C 2 B 3 A

b) (Allow Ss about two mins. to underline the adjectives in each text, then elicit whether each is an opinion adjective or a fact adjective.)

Adjectives used to describe objects:
A lovely, new, big, light, special
B elegant, pink and white, striped
C huge, polished, wooden, black, shiny

opinion adjectives: lovely, special, elegant
fact adjectives: new, big, light, pink and white, striped, huge, polished, wooden, black, shiny

3 (Read aloud the adjectives in the list and explain/elicit the meanings of any unknown words. Complete the task orally with the class, then in writing.)

Opinion	elegant, extraordinary
Size/Weight	long, heavy, light
Age	20th century, ancient, modern
Shape	round, rectangular, square
Pattern/Decoration	striped, carved, polka-dot
Colour	green, purple, red
Origin	Chinese, Irish, Indian
Material	plastic, crystal, paper
Special features	straps, stickers, handmade

4 (Explain/Elicit the meanings of any unknown words, then allow Ss two or three mins. to complete the task. Check Ss' answers around the class, and elicit which picture each description refers to.)

a) 1 beautiful Venetian ceramic
2 old-fashioned carved wooden
3 fantastic late 19th century multicoloured hand-woven
4 long brand-new oak

b) A = 4 B = 2 C = 3 D = 1

5 a) (Read the rubric aloud and complete the first task orally with the class.)

Key words: lost — sports bag — while staying at hotel — left it at gym — letter — manager — describing bag

b) zips ✓ shoulder strap ✓
wheels handles ✓
locks side pockets ✓

c) (Allow Ss about five mins. to write a short description of the bag. Check Ss' answers around the class.)

(Suggested answer)

It is a large multicoloured sports bag with several zips and side pockets. It is lightweight, rectangular in shape and made of nylon. It has a black shoulder strap as well as black handles.

Unit 9 - Describing Festivals/Events/Celebrations (pp. 56 - 59)

1 *(Elicit from Ss what sort of information might be included in a description of a festival, event or celebration, and help individual Ss to describe one they have attended. Explain that they are now going to listen to a description of a festival. Read the table aloud and explain/elicit the meanings of any unknown words. Then, Ss do the listening activity. Check Ss' answers around the class. Finally, ask individual Ss to describe the event.)*

Name of festival:	La Mercé festival	✓	Sardana festival	☐
Time:	at the end of the year	☐	at the end of September	✓
Reason:	to celebrate the patron saint of Barcelona	✓	to celebrate the end of summer	☐
Preparations:	costumes made musicians practise	✓ ✓	Spanish food prepared streets decorated	☐ ☐
Actual event:	sports events people dancing lots of parades	☐ ✓ ✓	people dress up acrobats perform tricks firework display	✓ ✓ ✓
Comments:	very disappointing	☐	spectacular	✓

2 *(Present the theory and the paragraph plan, then explain/elicit the meanings of any unknown words in the rubric. Help Ss to identify the key words to be underlined and elicit suitable answers to the questions.)*

a) **Key words:** travel magazine – descriptions – annual events – their country – you have attended – preparations – events on the actual day

1 A, C – because the rubric asks for a description of an **annual** event in **your** country.
2 B ✓   C ✓
3 mainly past tenses, because you are describing an **annual** event **you have attended**.

b) *(For questions 1 - 4, complete the task orally with the class. Then, ask individual Ss around the class to answer question 5.)*

1 A   3 B   5 (Ss' own answers)
2 A   4 A, C, E, F

c) *(Allow Ss about 4 mins. to skim the text and complete the task. Check Ss' answers. Explain/ Elicit the meanings of any unknown words in the text, then ask individual Ss to read the completed text aloud.)*

2 is usually held   9 practised
3 continues   10 were dressed
4 arrived   11 decided
5 had been put up   12 stood up
6 had been placed   13 waved
7 had been set up   14 rushed
8 served   15 exploded

Para 1: name, place/time, reason
Para 2: preparations
Para 3: description of actual event
Para 4: feelings, comments, final thoughts

d) *(Write the headings on the board and elicit suitable points from Ss to complete the table on the board. Individual Ss use the notes to talk about the Regatta and then copy the table into their books.)*

Para 1
• Royal Regatta • Henley • end of June
• teams of rowers compete for prizes
Para 2
• grandstands put up • deckchairs placed along river • tents set up • food/drinks served
• rowers practise
Para 3
• spectators watched races, had picnics
• during final, crowd cheered and waved
• firework display

Unit 9

Para 4
• sad event was over • it would be fun to take part in races

3 a) A 1 various   4 scary
       2 colourful   5 well-known
       3 creative   6 hand-carved
     B 1 disappointed 2 poor   3 dim
     C 1 glittering   2 Glamorous 3 lucky

b) A = main body
     B = conclusion
     C = introduction

4 *(Ss do the exercise orally, then assign it as written HW.)*

A ... Children make an effigy of Guy and buy fireworks with their pocket money. Big bonfires **are built** in gardens or at organised sites. In the evening, spectacular fireworks **are let off** and everyone eats baked potatoes. At the end of the evening, the effigy of Guy **is burnt**.

B The latest computers **are displayed** in a large hall and companies give away a lot of free software. Full-length feature films **are shown** in the auditorium. Everyone usually enjoys the event immensely.

5 *(Allow Ss three mins to skim the extracts and complete the task. Check Ss' answers round the class.)*

(Suggested answers)
1 B – a past event
   The writer felt happy because all the effort was worthwhile.

2 C – an annual event
   The writer feels that St Valentine's Day is a day for romantic people of all ages.
3 A – a past event
   The writer felt exhausted but delighted that the party had been a success.

6 a) *(Complete the task orally with the class, then explain/elicit the meanings of any unknown words.)*

1 D   3 B   5 B   7 D   9 D
2 B   4 D   6 B   8 B

b) *(Individual Ss make full sentences from the prompts. Elicit a suitable topic sentence for each paragraph. When satisfied that Ss can deal with the task successfully, assign it as written HW.)*

(Suggested answer)
    Many preparations are made for the Dominica Carnival. Everybody works enthusiastically to get ready for the carnival. Brightly-decorated floats are built and designers make colourful masks and costumes. Local musicians practise very hard for the big event, too. Then, the night before the carnival, people go to a lively street party.
    The day of the carnival is very exciting as the streets are filled with people dancing and singing to live music. Tourists line the streets to watch the fantastic parade and try the mouth-watering Caribbean food that is sold at street stalls. During all this a carnival queen is chosen and awarded a prize.

7 *(Read the items in the table aloud and explain/elicit the meanings of any unknown words. Then, Ss do the listening activity. Check Ss' answers around the class. Finally, ask individual Ss to describe the event using past tenses.)*
The event described is not an annual event.

Reason for celebration:		50th wedding anniversary	☐	25th wedding anniversary	✓
Place held:		hotel reception room	✓	large house	☐
Preparations:		sent invitations	✓	hired caterers	☐
		booked hotel rooms	✓	went to hairdresser's	☐
		cleaned the house	☐	ordered flowers	✓
Actual day:	Guests:	50	✓	500	☐
	Food:	three-course meal	✓	hot buffet	☐
	Music:	Sixties	✓	Seventies	☐
	Other:	party games	☐	speech	✓
Feelings:		parents had a wonderful time	✓	disappointed some family members didn't come	☐

8 *(Help Ss to identify the key words to be underlined and elicit suitable answers to the questions.)*

Key words: teacher – describe – wedding anniversary celebration – you recently attended – article – descriptions of preparations – activities on the actual day

1 C, B
2 I B II B III D IV D
3 *(Ss' own answers)* – *(Ss, in pairs discuss these questions for three mins. Go round the class and check Ss' answers, then ask some Ss to report back to the class.)*
4 Extract A is suitable because it describes the name and time of the celebration and the reason for celebrating.
Extract B is not suitable because it describes the actual day of the celebration.

9 *(When satisfied that Ss can deal with the task successfully, assign the exercise as written HW.)*

(Suggested answer)

Every anniversary is special to a married couple, but the twenty-fifth, or silver wedding anniversary, is a particularly important occasion. Last Saturday, it was my parents' silver wedding anniversary. My brother and I organised a huge party so that Mum and Dad could celebrate the big day in style.

Several weeks before the event we made a guest list and sent the invitations. We had to book hotel rooms for a few relatives who were coming from abroad, too. We ordered beautiful flower arrangements to decorate every table and chose some great dishes for the three-course meal. We kept the whole thing a surprise.

The party had a really lively atmosphere. There were more than fifty guests, and later in the evening, everyone got up and danced. The DJ played my dad's favourite music from the Sixties – I've never seen him dance so much!

It was lovely to see my parents having such a wonderful time. All the planning and preparation was certainly worth it.

Unit 10 - First-person Narratives (pp. 60 - 65)

1 *(Ask Ss to look at the pictures, and read questions 1-3. Play the cassette for Ss to listen to the story and put the pictures into the correct order, then prepare their answers to the questions. Elicit suitable answers, helping Ss where necessary.)*

a) 1 C 2 A 3 D 4 B
1 The driver, the instructor and the examiner.
2 The driver.
3 **(Suggested answer)**
"An Unforgettable Experience."

b) *(Ss' own answers)*

2 *(Present the theory and the paragraph plan. Help Ss to identify the key words in the rubric, then elicit answers to the questions.)*

Key words: local newspaper – story competition – story should start with: "I stood on the deck staring at the huge waves"

1 Readers of a local newspaper
2 B
3 A

3 a) *(Allow Ss two to three mins. to look at the picture and complete the task. Explain/Elicit the meaning of any unknown vocabulary, then ask individual Ss to read their answers aloud.)*

1 on a ship
2 cold and windy
3 a fire in the engine room
4 the ship reached the port
5 loudspeakers
  engine room
  lifeboat station
  cabin
  lifejackets

b) *(Allow Ss five or six mins. to read the text and underline the correct tenses. Elicit suitable answers, helping Ss where necessary. Explain/ Elicit the meaning of any words from the story which Ss still do not understand, then ask individual Ss to read aloud from the text including their answers. Then, give Ss about two mins. to label the paragraphs.)*

1 had left   5 ran   9 announced
2 stopped   6 showed   10 cheered
3 slowed   7 looked   11 moved
4 told   8 passed   12 was standing

Para 1: setting the scene
Paras 2 - 4: development of story
Para 5: end of story, feelings

Unit 10

c) *(Allow Ss about four mins. to read the text again and number the events in the correct order. Check Ss' answers. Then, help Ss to tell the story orally in the first person.)*

A 5	C 2	E 9	G 3	I 8
B 7	D 4	F 6	H 1	

d) *(Allow Ss about three mins. to fill in the correct adjectives. Check Ss' answers, then help individual Ss to make appropriate sentences.)*

1 huge   3 rough   5 solid
2 dark   4 tiny

(Ss' own answers)

4 a) *(Explain/Elicit the meaning of any unknown vocabulary in the rubrics and plot lines. Allow Ss three or four mins. to complete the task, then check Ss' answers. Ss, in pairs, then think of alternative plot lines. Check Ss' answers round the class, then ask some Ss to report back to the class.)*

1 B   2 A

b) *(Allow Ss four or five mins. to read the rubric and the plot line and number the events in the correct order. Then, help Ss to tell the story orally in the first person.)*

(Suggested answer)
As soon as I got off the train I knew this would be a special day in my life. As I was walking down the street, I found a wallet on the pavement. I put the wallet in my pocket and went to the job interview.
Unfortunately, I didn't get the job. I left the building very disappointed. It was then that I remembered the wallet. I opened it and looked inside. I found the owner's address, so I went to the owner to give it back. The owner was very rich. He was very happy to have his wallet back and he offered me a job.

b 3	d 8	f 2	h 7	j 4
c 5	e 9	g 10	i 6	

5 *(Allow Ss three or four mins. to read the extracts and fill in the gaps. Check Ss' answers. Explain/Elicit the meanings of any words Ss do not understand, then ask individual Ss to read the extracts aloud.)*

A 1 As soon as   4 Meanwhile
   2 Suddenly   5 Suddenly
   3 Before   6 eventually

B 1 As   3 Suddenly   5 then
   2 soon   4 At first   6 finally

6 a) *(Help Ss to match the phrases to the pictures. Then, Ss listen and check their answers.)*

D waves thundering and crashing
B shiny green leaves
A calm water
D salty sea spray
B smell of damp ferns
D white foamy water
A sparkling lights
A loud car horns

b) **picture A:** sight and hearing
   picture B: sight and smell
   picture D: sight, taste, touch and hearing

7 *(Present the theory on past tenses. Allow Ss three or four mins. to read the extract and underline the verbs. Check Ss' answers.)*

1 wasn't   8 went
2 thought   9 was
3 was   10 was standing
4 was rattling 11 saw
5 froze   12 was
6 heard   13 had got up
7 decided

8 *(Present the theory on narrative techniques. Allow Ss three or four mins. to complete the task and answer the questions. Check Ss' answers.)*

a) 1 C   2 A   3 B

b) 1 using the senses (to set the scene)
   2 using the senses to describe the weather and using direct speech
   3 referring to feelings/moods and addressing the reader directly
   A referring to feelings/moods and asking a rhetorical question
   B referring to feelings/moods and asking a rhetorical question
   C referring to feelings/moods and using direct speech

c) *(Elicit suggestions for beginnings and endings. Then, help Ss to complete the task orally and assign it as a written exercise.)*

(Suggested answers)
BEGINNING:
   Have you ever had one of those days when you just can't seem to do anything right? Well, for me, yesterday was one of those days.

ENDING:
   As I locked the door of the shop and set the alarm, I remembered what had happened earlier. Sighing, I said to myself, "Thank goodness today is over!"

9 *(Allow Ss four or five mins. to read the beginnings and complete the task. Check Ss' answers.)*

a) 4 is the least interesting because no writing techniques have been applied.

b) use(s) the senses   2, 5
use(s) direct speech   1, 2
address(es) the reader directly   3
refer(s) to feeling or moods   5

c) *(Elicit suggestions for beginnings, then allow Ss two or three mins. to complete the task. Check Ss' answers.)*

(Suggested answer)
   It was a bright and sunny Monday morning and I was cycling to school. As I was turning the corner, a dog ran in front of me and I crashed my bike into a tree. I was alright, but my bike was badly damaged. "Oh, dear!" I said out loud. "How am I going to pay for the repairs?"

10 a) *(Explain/Elicit the meanings of any unknown words in the rubric and questions. Help Ss to identify the key words, then elicit suitable answers to the questions.)*

Key words: popular magazine – short story competition – must end with: "It was the best day of my life."

1 Readers of a popular magazine
2 Me
3 C

b) *(Elicit from Ss what is happening in each picture. Then, read the plot line and allow Ss two mins. to put the sentences into the correct order. Check Ss' answers.)*

2 A woman stopped me.
4 I waved goodbye and left.
5 I arrived too late for the concert.
6 I saw the woman I had helped at the entrance of the concert hall.
3 I helped her change the tyre.
8 She got me a front-row seat.
1 I was driving to a concert.
9 After the concert I met the band.
7 She was the band's manager.

c) *(Allow Ss two or three mins. to complete the task. Check Ss' answers.)*

- a woman stopped me. I helped her change the tyre.
- waved goodbye and left.
- the woman I had helped at the entrance of the concert hall. She was the band's manager. She got me a front-row ticket.
- the band.

11 *(Help individual Ss to complete the task orally, using their answers from Ex. 10 and adding their own ideas where necessary. When satisfied that Ss can deal with the task successfully, assign it as written HW.)*

(Suggested answer)
   One night last year, as I was on my way to see my favourite rock band, 'Brand X', I saw a woman who needed help changing a flat tyre. Although it was raining heavily, I stopped to help her.
   I managed to change the tyre, although I got quite wet and dirty in the process. "Thank you so much. That was very kind of you," she said to me. I told her it was no trouble as I made my way back to my car and waved goodbye. I was a little worried that the delay would make me late for the concert.
   I was right. When I arrived at the concert hall, the doors were closed and I was very disappointed. Just as I was about to leave, I saw the woman I had helped at the entrance of the concert hall. I couldn't believe it when she said she was the band's manager and arranged for me to have a front-row seat. The concert was fantastic!
   Afterwards, I was invited backstage and I got to meet the band. Who would have thought that a good deed would pay off in such a delightful way? *It was the best day of my life.*

Unit 11 - Third-person Narratives (pp. 66 - 71)

(As a preparation for Ex. 1, elicit from Ss various key words and phrases which describe the scenes in the pictures. Write these on the board. Ss copy them into their notebooks.)

Suggested words/phrases: woke up, realised, late, rushed out, get taxi, elderly man, pushed, slammed door, reached airport, in time for flight, sat by window, read newspaper, sat next to him, embarrassed

1 *(Elicit the correct order of the pictures. Then, Ss do the listening task. Check Ss' answers. Elicit which picture each word/phrase describes. Then, help Ss to retell the story orally, using past tenses. They may use their notes to help them.)*

A – 4   C – 5   E – 1
B – 3   D – 2

(Ss' own answers)

2 *(Present the theory and the paragraph plan. Then read the rubric and the questions aloud. Elicit the key words to be underlined. Check Ss' answers.)*

Key words: popular magazine – short story competition – must begin with – "Are you sure it's safe?" Josh asked his friend.

1 Readers of the popular magazine.
2 B
3 B
4 "Are you sure it's safe?" Josh asked his friend.

3 a) *(Allow Ss three or four mins. to look at the picture and answer the questions. Check Ss' answers.)*

1 B   2 A   3 B   4 A   5 A   6 A

b) *(Allow Ss about four mins. to read the story, label the paragraphs and number the events in order. Check Ss' answers, then ask individual Ss to read aloud from the text.)*
Para 1: setting the scene
Paras 2 - 3: development of story
Para 4: end of story, feelings and comments

B **6** Marty grabbed Josh.
C **2** Josh started to cross the rope bridge.
D **1** Marty crossed the bridge safely.
E **4** Josh clung to the other rope.
F **7** Marty and Josh walked away from the bridge.
G **5** Josh moved carefully along the rope.

c) A Nasty Experience

4 a) *(Present the theory on adjectives and adverbs. Explain/Elicit the meaning of any unknown vocabulary, then allow Ss four or five mins. to complete the task. Check Ss' answers.)*

BIG: (great), massive, gigantic, huge, enormous
SMALL: miniature, tiny
BAD: evil, horrible, terrible, wicked
GOOD/NICE: (great), delightful, fabulous, pleasant, terrific, attractive
VERY: great, highly, extremely, remarkably, absolutely
WELL: happily, successfully, satisfactorily

b) *(Allow Ss two or three mins. to complete the task. Then, ask individual Ss to read their answers aloud.)*

1 delightful/fabulous/pleasant/terrific
2 great/fabulous/terrific
3 attractive
4 happily
5 massive/gigantic/huge/enormous
6 tiny
7 extremely

5 *(Explain that the verbs in the list are introductory verbs to be used instead of said. Allow Ss two or three mins. to complete the task. Check Ss' answers.)*

2 promised   4 screamed   6 admitted
3 reminded   5 threatened

6 a) *(Present the theory on similes. Explain/elicit the meaning of any unknown words in the exercise. Check Ss' answers around the class.)*

2 G   4 J   6 A   8 F   10 I
3 B   5 E   7 H   9 D

b) *(Explain/elicit the meaning of any unknown words, then allow Ss about two mins. to complete the rest of the task. Check Ss' answers.)*

2 as black as   4 as busy as
3 a baby   5 a leaf

Unit 11

7 a) *(Allow Ss two or four mins. to complete the table. Check Ss' answers.)*

1	excited	5	bored
2	worried	6	scared
3	depressed	7	angry
4	sure		

b) *(Read out the adjectives in the list. Ss read what each person says and match the speakers to how they feel. Check Ss' answers, then Ss make sentences as in the example.)*

2 B   3 D   4 C   5 A   6 E

2 She was amazed because it was a very tall building.
3 He was worried because he didn't know if everything was okay.
4 She was amused because it was a really funny joke.
5 She was confused because she wasn't sure what to do.
6 She was excited because she was really looking forward to her holiday.

8 a) *(Allow Ss two or three mins. to complete the task and answer the questions. Check Ss' answers.)*

A 1 golden   3 beautiful
   2 colourful 4 Eagerly
B 1 extremely 3 unbelievable
   2 warm   4 wonderful

b) 1 A – A beginning   B – An ending
2 In para A the writer feels excited.
In para B the writer feels tired.
He/She also feels relieved.

9 *(Allow Ss two or three mins. to complete the task. Check Ss' answers.)*

1 angrily   3 silently   5 excitedly
2 rudely   4 nervously   6 hurriedly

10 *(Present the theory on present and past participles. Then, read the first two examples and ask Ss to underline the words closing and worried and identify them as present or past participles. Allow Ss four or five mins. to complete the task. Check Ss' answers.)*

3 Falling to his knees, he started crying.
4 Whispering, they walked up the stairs.
5 Frightened, he realised no one would help him.
6 Standing at the edge of the cliff, he watched the magnificent sunset.
7 Covered with a warm blanket, she finally felt safe.
8 Annoyed, she gathered her things and left the room.

11 a) *(Explain/Elicit the meaning of any unknown vocabulary, then allow Ss four or five mins. to put the paragraphs into the correct order and answer the questions. Check Ss' answers.)*

A 3   B 1   C 2

1 Sharon is the main character. She is on a plane.
2 The plane is about to crash.
3 She is very frightened.
4 The main body.

b) (Suggested answer)

After what seemed like hours, Sharon managed to crawl onto the beach. She was shivering with cold. She looked around her and felt exhausted but relieved. It had been a truly terrifying experience!

12 a) *(Allow Ss three or four mins. to complete the task and answer the questions. Check Ss' answers.)*

1 b   2 a   3 c

3 C is the worst pair because there are no writing techniques

b) 1 direct speech, referring to feelings or moods
2 addressing the reader directly, referring to feelings
3 —

a direct speech
b direct speech
c —

(Suggested answers)

"Hey, let's go camping for the weekend." Joe said. His friends all agreed that it was a good idea, but little did they know what was in store for them.

Early the next morning, as they were angrily taking down their tents, they all looked at Joe. "What" he said, "I didn't know there were grizzly bears in the forest!"

35

Unit 12a

13 a) *(Elicit from Ss what is happening in each picture, then read the questions aloud and elicit appropriate answers around the class.)*

(Suggested answers)
1 Summer
2 They were a family on holiday.
3 They were spending the day at the beach.
4 Yes, I do.
5 Four o'clock in the afternoon.
6 The tide had come in.
7 Yes.
8 They probably felt afraid.
9 The captain of a boat passing by.
10 They probably felt relieved.
11 They probably said, "Thank you. You saved our lives."

b) *(Allow Ss two mins. to read the notes and put them in the order they happened. Then, help Ss to retell the story.)*

A 3   B 2   C 5   D 1   E 4

14 *(Help Ss identify the key words in the rubric and refer them to the plan on p. 66. Check that Ss can complete the task orally, then assign it as written HW.)*

Key words: your teacher – story – must end with: "They decided to be more careful next time."

(Suggested answer)

It was a hot sunny day last summer when the Hardy family took a trip to the seaside. After walking for a while they found a great spot on a deserted beach.

"It's like paradise!" Mrs Hardy said, as she and Mr Hardy settled down to sunbathe. The children ran off happily to play and swim.

Later that afternoon, after spending a wonderful day at the seaside, they decided to leave. They started crossing the rocks. Soon they realised they were trapped as the sea was too far in. "Oh, my goodness!" exclaimed Mr Hardy. "The tide is coming in!" They were extremely frightened.

Just then, they saw a small tourist boat not far away. They started shouting and waving their arms to attract the attention of the people on the boat. Luckily, the captain of the boat saw them and came over to pick them up.

When the boat arrived at the harbour, they all felt incredibly relieved. "I don't know what we'd have done if you hadn't arrived," said Mr Hardy to the captain. "Thank you very much." They decided to be more careful next time!

Unit 12a - News Reports (pp. 72 - 77)

1 *(Read the table aloud and explain/elicit the meaning of any unknown words. Ss do the listening task. Then, check Ss' answers around the class. Finally, ask individual Ss to describe what happened.)*

Date:	Tuesday night	✓	last night	☐
Place:	island of St Finn	✓	island of Pepco	☐
Main Events:	oil tanker hit rocks	✓	oil tanker exploded	☐
	chemicals leaked into sea	☐	oil leaked into sea	✓
	seabirds, wildlife harmed	✓	seabirds, wildlife unharmed	☐
Comments and action to be taken:	beach now closed	☐	beach being cleaned	✓
	residents angry	✓	residents calm	☐
	first time faced such a situation	☐	one of worst situations ever faced	✓

(Ss' own answers)

Unit 12a

2 *(Present the theory and the paragraph plan. Then, read the rubric aloud and explain/elicit the meaning of any unknown words. Allow Ss two or three mins. to underline the key words and answer the questions. Check Ss' answers.)*

Key words: news report – young child – received award – bravery – reason award given – information about prize-giving ceremony

1 B
2 A, C - because the rubric states that it was a young child who received an award for bravery
3 A , C
4 paragraph 1
5 the final paragraph
6 Short forms and colloquial language may be used in the final paragraph, if they are part of sb's comments in direct speech. Chatty descriptions should not be used.

3 a) *(Check that Ss understand the headings, then allow Ss two or three mins. to skim the article and label the paragraphs. Check Ss' answers. Finally, ask individual Ss to read the news report aloud.)*

Para 2: reason for award
Para 3: description of ceremony
Para 4: people's comments

b) (verbs in the passive to be underlined)

was presented (para 1)
was trapped (para 2)
was followed (para 3)
was attended (para 3)
had been recognised (para 4)

(reporting verbs:)
commented ⎫ they are in the last paragraph
saying   ⎬ because this paragraph
pointed out ⎭ includes people's comments

c) 2 bravery   7 stayed
    3 came   8 rescue
    4 saved   9 informal
    5 risked   10 attended
    6 trapped   11 owed

(Ss' own answers)

4 *(Present the theory on headlines, then help Ss to complete the task, first orally, then in writing.)*

2 Fans injured at match
3 Sixty-year-old man shot by car thieves
4 Climbers reach top of Everest
5 Brilliant season for Manchester United
6 Young girl rescues brother from kidnappers

5 *(Read out the headlines then, Ss in pairs complete the task. Check Ss' answers.)*

a) 1 a   2 d   3 c

The extra headline is **b**

b) (Suggested answer)
More than ten people were injured yesterday during the semi-final of the Champion's League competition, held at Brickgate Stadium.

6 *(Read out the prompts, then Ss in pairs complete the task. Check Ss' answers, then individual Ss read out their paragraphs. Elicit various headlines from Ss and write them on the board. Ss can choose the best for each news report.)*

1 A valuable Renoir painting was stolen late last night from the Terrence Wagner Museum. The painting is worth over £2 million and has been in the museum since 1983.
2 The new space station Hermes was successfully launched from Cape Kennedy yesterday. It will remain in orbit around the earth for the next eight months.

(Suggested answer)
Headlines: 1 → Valuable Renoir Stolen
              2 → Hermes In Orbit

7 *(Allow Ss two mins. to complete the task. Check Ss' answers orally in class.)*

1 Mrs Gingelli gave birth to seven baby boys, **who** are all said to be doing well.
2 An elephant, **which** escaped from Janneto's Circus, was caught yesterday.
3 Doctor Tina White, **whose** discovery will help save many lives, was awarded a prize.
4 The police have closed the road **where** the accident happened.
5 Ten people were injured yesterday **when** a bus overturned in Westville.

8 *(Ss in pairs fill in the correct words. Check Ss' answers while individual Ss read out their answers. Explain/Elicit the meaning of any word Ss still do not understand.)*

37

Unit 12a

a) 1 1) struck 3) damage
2) casualties 4) homeless
2 5) broken into 7) witness
6) alarm 8) armed
3 9) Rescue workers 12) debris
10) survivors 13) cause
11) trapped
4 14) Residents 17) goals
15) celebrating 18) championship
16) victory

b) 3 = an accident
1 = a natural disaster
4 = a sports event
2 = a crime

c) A 3   B 4   C 2   D 1

9 *(Present the theory and explain/elicit the meaning of any unknown words. Allow Ss three or four mins. to complete the task. Check Ss' answers.)*

1 b, 2 a

a) 1,b → from a news report
2,a → from a narrative
b) Yes, they do.
c) 1, b
d) 2, a

10 *(Allow Ss three or four mins. to complete the task. Check Ss' answers and explain/elicit the meaning of any words which Ss still do not understand.)*

1 seriously injured
2 praised
3 comment on
4 furious
5 suffering from exhaustion
6 take action
7 admitted responsibility for
8 presented with
9 denied all knowledge of
10 refused to cooperate with

11 *(Allow Ss three mins. to complete the task, then check Ss' answers.)*

1 One of the museum's most valuable paintings was destroyed by a fire.
2 The writer of the best story will be given a prize.
3 The lost child was found in the mountains by a rescue team.
4 The east coast of the island was hit by heavy storms late last night.

12 *(Explain/Elicit the meaning of any unknown words and complete the first answer with the class. Allow Ss two or three mins. to skim the text and complete the remainder of the task. Ask individual Ss to read the completed introduction and conclusion aloud. Finally, help individual Ss to make full sentences for the main body using the sketches and prompts. Ss then write the main body. Check Ss' answers.)*

1 was made   4 was chosen
2 was closed   5 want
3 left   6 noticed

(Suggested answer)

The bomb had been hidden in a large shopping bag and left under a bench on platform 2. It was reported by a passenger at 7:00 am.
The police immediately evacuated the station while explosives experts were called. Nobody was hurt in the incident.

13 *(Allow Ss three mins. to complete the task. Individual Ss read out their answers.)*

1 At the press conference, the Mayor **promised** that he would do everything in his power to help the victims of the earthquake.
2 The manager of the factory, Mr G Graham, **refused** to say anything until he had all the facts.
3 When he was arrested, Mr Smith **denied** taking/having taken the money or the gold.
4 Doctor Godfrey **informed** us that the situation was serious but that they were doing all they could.
5 Headmaster Mr P Brown **commented** that it was a great achievement for their students and he was proud of them all.
6 The Prime Minister **announced** that the price of petrol would increase by 2p per litre from midnight on Tuesday.

14 *(Explain the task, then allow Ss about two mins. to fill in the plan. Check Ss' answers. Individual Ss use the completed plan to talk about the event.)*

Summary of Event
• Who: pop singer *Any Wonder*.
• Where: 5 Brunel Street, East London
• When: Friday, 20th June

(Ss' own answers)

15 **a)** *(Read the rubric aloud and explain/elicit the meaning of any unknown words. Allow Ss two or three mins. to underline the key words and answer the questions. Check Ss' answers.)*

Key words: news report – opening of *Shake!* club – detailed description of event – suitable headline

1. A news report (for *Music Echo* magazine)
2. The readers of the magazine you work for.
3. Yes.
4. passive voice ✓ formal linking words ✓ variety of reporting verbs ✓

b) *(When satisfied that Ss can deal with the task successfully, assign it as written HW.)*

(Suggested answer)
Shake's Opening Night

The long-awaited opening of *Shake!* music club, at 5 Brunel Street, East London, took place on Friday 20th June. The main event of the opening was a live performance by the pop singer *Any Wonder*.

At six o'clock fans of the popular singer had already started queuing outside the club. *Any Wonder* arrived in a black limousine around 8:15 pm and, as expected, signed autographs. The club opened its doors at 9pm and an hour later *Any Wonder* was on stage.

The performance was excellent and fans were delighted. Club owner Martin Lowe said, "I hope the club will be a great success."

Unit 12b - Reviews (pp. 78 - 81)

1 *(Allow Ss two or three mins. to look at the pictures and prepare their answers to the questions, then ask individual Ss to report back to the class.)*

a) (Suggested answer)
I'd rather read the book because books are usually more interesting than films.

b) 1 film   2 book

c) (Suggested answer)
types of books: mysteries, science-fiction, biographies, novels, etc
types of films: comedies, thrillers, action films, etc

d) *(Ss' own answers)*

e) (Suggested answers)
It's a very entertaining read. It's a great book. Don't miss it. It is well worth seeing etc.

2 *(Present the theory and the paragraph plan, then read the rubric and the questions aloud. Explain/ Elicit the meanings of any unknown words. Help Ss to identify the key words, then Ss complete the tasks. Check Ss' answers.)*

Key words: editor of magazine you work for – you write – review about book – recently read – brief summary of plot – why readers enjoy it

1. Readers of the magazine.
2. A, C, E, F, G, I J
3. present tenses.

3 **a)** *(Ask Ss if they have read the "The Hound of the Baskervilles". If yes ask them to tell the class the summary of it and whether they liked it or not. Allow Ss three or four mins. to skim the review and label the paragraphs. Check Ss' answers.)*

Para 1: background information
Para 2: main points of plot
Para 3: general comments
Para 4: recommendation

b) *(Allow Ss a further four or five mins. to read the review again and answer the questions. Explain/ Elicit the meanings of any words they do not understand. Finally, ask individual Ss to read their answers aloud.)*

1. Para 4. I thoroughly recommend ...
2. Para 2. No, she doesn't.
3. Para 1.
4. Para 3. thrilling moments, creates tension with unexpected twists and vivid descriptions, dark atmosphere, silent, evil presence of legendary hound, dominates story throughout
5. passive voice; variety of adjectives; complex sentences

4 **a)** *(Explain/Elicit the meaning of any unknown vocabulary. Allow Ss four or five mins. to complete the task. Check Ss' answers.)*

Unit 12b

Books
The book/novel was written by ...
It is beautifully/poorly/badly written.
It is a highly entertaining read.
It's a bore to read.

Films
The film is directed by ...
The cast is excellent/awful/unconvincing.
The script is dull/exciting.
Don't miss it. It is well worth seeing.
It's bound to be a box-office hit.
Wait until it comes out on video.

Both
The film/book tells the story of ...
The film/story is set in ...
It is a comedy/horror film/love story.
The story concerns/is about/begins ...
The plot is (rather) boring/thrilling.
The plot has an unexpected twist.
It is rather long/boring/confusing/slow.
It has a tragic/dramatic end.
I wouldn't recommend it because ...
I highly/thoroughly recommend it.

b) *(Allow Ss two or three mins. to complete the task. Check Ss' answers.)*

story set in ...
The book tells the story of ...
The story begins ...
The Hound of the Baskervilles is a highly entertaining read ...

5 *(Allow Ss three or four mins. to read the sentences and choose the correct item. Explain/Elicit the meaning of any unknown vocabulary, while checking Ss' answers.)*

1 role
2 audience
3 written
4 twist
5 tragic
6 cast
7 based on
8 special effects
9 dull read
10 tells the story

6 a) *(Allow Ss three or four mins. to read both columns and match them. Check Ss' answers.)*

1 D   3 A   5 B   7 C
2 G   4 H   6 E   8 F

b) *(Allow Ss two or three mins. to complete the task. Check Ss' answers.)*

1 excellent, superb, fantastic, fascinating, entertaining
2 thrilling
3 hilarious, entertaining, amusing
4 moving, touching
5 dull
6 terrible, awful, dreadful

c) *(Allow Ss two or three mins. to complete the task. Check Ss' answers by asking individual Ss to read their sentences aloud.)*

(Suggested answers)
Lethal Weapon is a thrilling action film.
Home Alone is a hilarious comedy.
Oliver Twist is a touching story. etc

7 *(Allow Ss two or three mins. to complete the task. Check Ss' answers.)*

2 I thoroughly recommend *20,000 Leagues Under the Sea*. It is an exciting and thrilling read.
3 I wouldn't recommend *Sleep Well*. It is an extremely dull film.
4 *Stuart Little* is bound to be a box-office hit. It is a superb film.

8 *(Present the theory and explain/elicit the meaning of any unknown vocabulary. Allow Ss three or four mins. to complete the task. Check Ss' answers.)*

The story is about a young woman named Emily **who** is a private detective. She is hired by a mysterious lady **whose** uncle disappeared in Brazil. Emily's assignment takes her to Rio de Janeiro **where** she meets a strange man called David Travis. The man takes her on a dangerous journey **which** eventually leads them into the heart of the Amazon Rainforest.

9 a) *(Read the rubric and the questions aloud. Explain/Elicit the meanings of any unknown words, then Ss underline the key words and complete the tasks.)*

Key words: magazine – readers – reviews – films – recently seen – of interest to other people

1 Readers of the film magazine.
2 A, C, D, E, F

b) *(Allow Ss four or five mins. to read the review. Explain/Elicit the meaning of any unknown vocabulary, then Ss complete the task. Check Ss' answers.)*

Para 1: background information (title, type of film, name of director, names of actors and the characters they portray)
Para 2: main points of the plot
Para 3: general comments
Para 4: recommendation

Writer's recommendation: "I throughly recommend this film. Don't miss it."

(Suggested answer)
I would definitely recommend *Armagedon*. It is well worth seeing.

10 a) *(Read the rubric and the questions aloud. Explain/Elicit the meaning of any unknown vocabulary. Help Ss to identify the key words, then Ss decide on a certain film to be discussed. Then they ask the question. Individual Ss answer the questions. Check Ss' answers.)*

Key words: your teacher – write – film review – school magazine – write review – main points of the plot – general comments – acting – directing – plot – recommendation

1 My teacher. Present tenses.
2 passive voice; variety of adjectives; complex sentences
3 **(Suggested answers)**
   a) An animated comedy, b) Rob Minkoff, c) Hugh Laurie, Geena Davis, Jonathan Lipnicki and the voice of Michael J. Fox, d) Hugh Laurie and Geena Davis → Mr and Mrs Little, Jonathan Lipnicki → their son George, Michael J. Fox → the voice of Stuart Little, e) the film is about a couple who adopt a mouse to keep their son company
4 • family goes to orphanage to adopt a little boy but adopt a mouse instead
   • the son isn't happy because he would have preferred a real brother
   • The family cat tries to get rid of Stuart Little. The acting is excellent. The computer animation is convincing. Don't miss it!

b) *(Help Ss to compose their review orally using their answers from ex 10a. When satisfied that Ss can deal with the task successfully, assign it as written HW.)*

(Suggested answer)
Stuart Little
Stuart Little, an animated film directed by Rob Minkoff, takes place in New York City. The main characters are Mr and Mrs Little, played by Hugh Laurie and Geena Davis, their son George, played by Jonathan Lipnicki and, of course, the adorable mouse Stuart, whose voice is provided by Michael J. Fox.

The story begins when Mr and Mrs Little go to an orphanage to adopt a little brother for their son George. At the orphanage they meet Stuart, a tiny mouse, and are so charmed by him that they decide to adopt him. George, however, isn't pleased as he would have preferred a real brother. The family cat, Snowbell, along with other cats in the neighbourhood, have plans to get rid of Stuart forever!

The cast is excellent and Michael J. Fox is perfect as the voice of Stuart Little. With the use of computer animation, Stuart looks more like a real mouse than a cartoon mouse, convincing viewers that Stuart is a miniature actor. The combination of computer animation and live action is superb.

Stuart Little is a wonderful film for the whole family. The cute little mouse will have all members of the family laughing in their seats. Don't miss it!

Unit 13 - "For and Against" Essays (pp. 82 - 87)

1 a) *(Explain what is meant by* **pros** *and* **cons**, *then elicit suitable points from Ss around the class.)*

(Suggested answers)
Pros
The service can be very fast.
There can be lots of dishes to choose from.
The prices can be fairly reasonable.
Its relaxing atmosphere can make you enjoy your meal.

Cons
The service can be very slow.
There may not be much variety of dishes.
The restaurant can be very expensive.
The music can be so loud that it can drive you crazy.

Unit 13

b) *(Read the list of points aloud and ensure that Ss understand each point. Ss listen to the cassette and tick the comments mentioned. Check answers around the class and elicit whether each point is an advantage or a disadvantage.)*

(Points to be ticked)
A fun to eat out (advantage)
B not as tiring as cooking (advantage)
D expensive (disadvantage)
E unhealthy (disadvantage)

2 *(Present the theory and the paragraph plan. Check that Ss understand the rubric and the questions, then help Ss identify the key words.)*

Key words: your teacher — essay — arguments for and against travelling by boat

1 A "for and against" essay
2 No, because discursive essays are written in a formal style.
3 **(Points to be ticked)**
   1 – pro
   2 – con
   4 – con
   5 – pro

(Ss' own answers)

3 a) *(Allow Ss two or three mins. to skim the text and label the paragraphs. Check Ss' answers, then ask individual Ss to suggest alternative topic sentences.)*

Para 1: present topic
Para 2: arguments for
Para 3: arguments against
Para 4: opinion

• The writer believes that travelling by boat is a very enjoyable experience.

(Suggested answer)
• There are many points in favour of travelling by boat.
  On the other hand, travelling by boat has certain drawbacks.

b) *(Allow Ss three or four mins. to read the text again. Elicit suitable points to help Ss complete the table. Present the list of linking words, then ask individual Ss to use these and the table of points to talk about the topic.)*

Para 2	**FOR** **Arguments** 2) cheaper than other forms of travel 3) safe alternative to cars and planes **Justifications/Examples** a boat ticket usually costs less than a plane ticket fewer accidents at sea than in the air or on the roads
Para 3	**AGAINST** **Arguments** 1) usually takes much longer than other forms of travel 2) can be very unpleasant when the weather is bad or the sea is rough **Justifications/Examples** can be tiring uncomfortable or even frightening

(Ss' own answers)

4 *(Allow Ss three or four mins. to complete the task. Check Ss' answers, then explain/elicit the meaning of any vocabulary in the text which Ss still do not understand.)*

words to be replaced:
To begin with   → In the first place
Furthermore   → Secondly
For example   → For instance
Finally   → Thirdly
However   → On the other hand
As a result   → For this reason
In addition   → Moreover
All things considered → To sum up

a) To begin with, Furthermore, Finally, In addition
b) For example, As a result
c) However
d) All things considered

5 *(Explain/Elicit the meaning of any unknown vocabulary, then allow Ss two or three mins. to complete the task. Check Ss' answers.)*

1 Besides   3 in favour of   5 For instance
2 argue that   4 Even though

6 *(Explain/Elicit the meaning of any unknown vocabulary, then allow Ss two or three mins. to read the paragraph and complete the task. Check Ss' answers.)*

Unit 13

1 To begin with
2 Secondly
3 therefore
4 Finally

7 a) *(Present the theory and explain the task. Allow Ss three or four mins. to read the extract and complete the task in pairs. Check Ss' answers, explain/elicit the meanings of any unknown words and ask individual Ss to read the extract aloud.)*

    2 However, there are many arguments against using the Internet.

b) Arguments against using the Internet

- spend hours and hours sitting in front of a computer screen
- can be very expensive
- requires a lot of patience

8 a) *(Explain/Elicit the meaning of any unknown words in the table, then allow Ss three or four mins. to match the items and identify whether each point is "for" or "against". Check Ss' answers. Ask individual Ss to form appropriate sentences orally; then Ss repeat the task as a written exercise.)*

1 d – for
2 b – for
3 a – against
4 c – against

b)   To begin with, modelling can be an exciting career. For example, models usually travel to interesting places and often meet famous people. What is more, modelling gives you the opportunity to earn a lot of money as designers and fashion magazines are willing to pay high fees for popular models.

    First of all, models must constantly watch what they eat since they are expected to stay thin so that they look good all the time. Moreover, models have no privacy because reporters are always chasing them.

9 *(Present the theory, then explain/elicit the meaning of any unknown vocabulary in the extracts. Allow Ss three or four mins. to complete the task. Check Ss' answers.)*

A → beginning → addresses the reader directly/ asks a rhetorical question
B → ending → uses a quotation
C → beginning → asks a rhetorical question
D → ending → addresses the reader directly/ uses a quotation

10 a) *(Read the topic sentences aloud and help Ss to suggest suitable supporting sentences. Check Ss' answers, then Ss in pairs expand those into a full paragraph. Individual Ss read their answers aloud.)*

(Suggested answers)

1
- very demanding, as doctors often have to work long hours
- stressful, because doctors have to deal with emergencies every day

2
- learn from educational programmes, such as documentaries
- a cheap form of entertainment

3
- no privacy, because they are followed everywhere by reporters and fans
- lonely, because they do not know who their real friends are

1 ....To start with, doctors have to study all their lives in order to keep up with the latest medical developments. Secondly, the job is very demanding as doctors often have to work long hours. Furthermore, it is stressful because doctors have to deal with emergencies every day.

2 ...In the first place it helps us keep up to date with current news. In addition, we learn from educational programmes such as documentaries. Moreover, it is a cheap form of entertainment.

3 ...Firstly, they are never home because they travel all over the world giving concerts. Also, they have no privacy, because they are followed everywhere by reporters and fans. Lastly, they feel lonely because they do not know who their real friends are.

b) *(Read the quotations aloud and explain/elicit the meaning of any unknown words. Elicit which quotation matches each topic. Ask individual Ss to suggest appropriate endings using the quotations; Ss may then repeat the task as a written exercise.)*

a 3   b 1   c 2

(Suggested answers)

a) All in all, I believe that there are more disadvantages than advantages to being a famous rock star. After all, as Keith Richards once said, "Everybody wants to be famous until they are."

43

Unit 13

b) All things considered, being a doctor has both advantages and disadvantages. Perhaps that is what British surgeon A. Dickson Wright meant when he said, "We are humble men in our profession. We do our best."

c) In conclusion, although there are many points against watching television, I believe there are certainly arguments in its favour. After all, as British playwright, Dennis Potter, once said, "Television! The entertainment which flows like tap water."

11 *(Complete the task orally with the class, then assign it as written HW.)*

(Suggested answers)

1 Firstly, there are a number of exotic holiday destinations where the climate is hot all year round. Secondly, holiday-makers can take advantage of cheap flights and accommodation during the winter, since fewer people travel at this time of year.

2 For one thing, it is extremely dangerous. For example, firefighters risk their lives every time they enter a burning building.

3 To start with, it can be very expensive. Dog food and visits to the vet can cost a lot of money. Furthermore, looking after a dog can be tiring. For instance, you have to take it for regular walks and give it a lot of attention.

12 a) *(Ss discuss the questons in pairs. Monitor Ss' performance, prompting where necessary, then ask Ss to present their ideas to the class.)*

- *(Ss' own answers)*

   (Suggested answers)
- **Advantages**
  cheap
  travel fast
  environmentally-friendly
  can park easily

  Disadvantages
  dangerous - often have accidents
  drivers do not take care of cyclists
  tiring

- Cycling in the country is more relaxing because there is no heavy traffic or crowded streets. You can enjoy the scenery without breathing in car fumes.

- I think more people should cycle to work because cycling is a good way keep fit. Also, they would not feel so stressed trying to find a parking place to park their car.

b) *(Read the rubric and the questions aloud. Explain/Elicit the meaning of any unknown words and help Ss to identify the key words in the rubric, then elicit suitable answers to the questions.)*

Key words: health and fitness magazine – advantages and disadvantages – cycling as a form of transport – article

1 A "for and against" essay.
2 A – your opinion.
3 In the main body (para 2 and para 3).
4 In the conclusion.

c) *(Allow Ss two or three mins. to complete the task. Check Ss' answers.)*

2 ✓ D   7 ✓ A
4 ✓ A   8 ✓ D
5 ✓ D

d) *(Allow Ss two or three mins. to match the items. Check Ss' answers, then help Ss to form appropriate sentences orally.)*

A – 4   C – 1   E – 8
B – 7   D – 5   F – 2

(Suggested answers)

1 Cycling is an inexpensive form of transport **since** you do not have to spend money on things such as petrol or costly repairs.
2 Fumes from cars and lorries can damage your health. **For example**, in some cities the fumes are so bad that cyclists have to wear masks to protect them from pollution.
3 Cycling helps you to stay fit **because** it is a good form of exercise, particularly for the legs, heart and lungs.
4 Cycling on busy roads is not very safe, **as** drivers do not always give way to cyclists.
5 Cycling is an environmentally-friendly way to travel **because** it does not create air pollution.
6 Bicycles are unsuitable for long journeys **since** there is a limit to the distance a cyclist can reasonably travel in one day.

13 *(Help Ss to complete the task orally. When satisfied that Ss can deal with the task successfully, assign it as written HW.)*

(Suggested answer)

Most people own or have owned a bicycle. Yet how practical and beneficial is cycling when compared to other means of transport?

There are many advantages to cycling. To start with, cycling is an inexpensive form of transport, since you do not have to spend money on things such as petrol or costly repairs. What is more, cycling helps you to stay fit, because it is a good form of exercise, particularly for the legs, heart and lungs. Finally, cycling is an environmentally-friendly way to travel since it does not create air pollution.

On the other hand, cycling also has certain disadvantages. For one thing, the fumes from cars and lorries are bad for your health. For example, in some cities the fumes are so bad that cyclists have to wear masks to protect them from the pollution. Secondly, cycling on busy roads is not very safe as drivers do not always give way to cyclists. Finally, bicycles are unsuitable for long journeys since there is a limit to the distance a cyclist can reasonably travel in one day.

All things considered, while there are some disadvantages to cycling, as a form of transport it is both enjoyable and good for you. Why don't you give it a try?

Unit 14a - Opinion Essays (pp. 78-83)

1 *(Read the viewpoints and reasons aloud and explain/elicit the meaning of any unknown vocabulary. Ss listen and complete the task. Check Ss' answers. Ask Ss around the class to say which points they agree/disagree with.)*

A 2   B 3   C 1

(Ss' own answers)

2 *(Present the theory and the paragraph plan, then read the rubric and the questions aloud. Explain/ Elicit the meaning of any unknown vocabulary and help Ss to underline the key words. Ss complete the task. Check Ss' answers.)*

Key words: English and Maths are more important subjects than Art and Music – teacher – essay – giving your opinion – reasons to support your view(s)

1 My teacher.
2 No, I shouldn't, because opinion essays should be written in formal style.
3 B
4 B, C, D
5 *(Ss' own answers)*
6 **English and Maths**
   - tools to deal with everyday matters
   - help you communicate clearly
   - necessary in order to find a job

   Art and Music
   - provide well-rounded education
7 *(Ss' own answers)*

3 a) *(Check that Ss understand the headings, then allow Ss two or three mins. to skim the article and label the paragraphs. Check Ss' answers.)*

Para 1: subject & opinion
Para 2: first viewpoint & examples
Para 3: second viewpoint & examples
Para 4: opposing viewpoint(s)
Para 5: restate opinion

b) *(Allow Ss four or five mins. to read the essay again and prepare their answers. Discuss these answers with the class, then explain/elicit the meaning of any words which Ss still do not understand. Finally, ask individual Ss to read aloud from the text.)*

First Viewpoint
In the first place, when you know how to read, write and do simple calculations, you have the tools required in order to deal with everyday matters.

Reasons/Examples
- For example, being able to read and write can help you communicate and express yourself clearly.
- Moreover, you need basic maths for such daily chores as doing your shopping, paying your bills and managing your money.

Second Viewpoint
Furthermore, it is essential to have a good knowledge of English and Maths in order to find even the simplest job.

Unit 14a

Reason/Example
Reading, writing and mathematical skills are the minimum requirements that most employers demand.

Linking words/phrases to introduce viewpoints:
in the first place, furthermore

Linking words/phrases to introduce opposing viewpoint:
on the other hand
The writer agrees with the statement.

(Ss' own answers)

4 *(Read aloud the items in the list and elicit which category each belongs to.)*

1	**To list points:** firstly, to begin with, for one thing, lastly, secondly
2	**To add more points:** also, moreover, apart from this, in addition, furthermore
3	**To introduce opposing viewpoints:** although, on the other hand, however, nonetheless, while
4	**To introduce examples/reasons:** for example, such as, therefore, in other words, in particular, for instance, because, since
5	**To conclude:** to sum up, all things considered, taking everything into account

5 *(Allow Ss three or four mins. to complete the task. Check Ss' answers, then explain/elicit the meaning of any unknown vocabulary.)*

(Suggested answers)

A 1 However
    2 To begin with
    3 Furthermore

B 1 To sum up
    2 because
    3 Although

6 *(Allow Ss two or three mins. to complete the task. Check Ss' answers, then explain/elicit the meaning of any unknown vocabulary.)*

2 For example
3 What is more,
4 Secondly
5 since

7 *(Allow Ss four mins. to read the paragraph, then in pairs discuss the answers to questions a to c. Check Ss' answers.)*

a) The main idea of the paragraph is that there are certain disadvantages to having your own car. This is included in the first sentence of the paragraph.

b) Firstly, cars ...... basis.
Therefore, ... condition.
Moreover, ... stressful.
For example ...... time-consuming.

c) Linking words/phrases: **on the other hand** → nonetheless, **firstly** → for one thing, **therefore** → in other words, **moreover** → in addition to this, **for example** → for instance

8 *(Read the topic sentences aloud, then Ss, in groups think of appropriate supporting sentences. Go round the class and check Ss' answers, then Ss report back to the class.)*

(Suggested answers)

1 a) Firstly, they might be influenced by the violence they watch on TV.
   b) Moreover, they might become inactive and antisocial.
2 a) For example, a child who has to exercise and feed their pet every day is likely to become more mature and reliable.
   b) Moreover, children who have pets usually become more caring and sensitive than those children who do not have pets.
3 a) To begin with, there is a wide choice of things to do for entertainment.
   b) Secondly, you have the opportunity to meet a lot of different people.

9 *(Present the useful expressions and the example. Allow Ss three or four mins. to complete the task. Check Ss' answers by asking individual Ss to read their completed sentences aloud.)*

(Suggested answers)

2 I strongly believe that all students should learn a foreign language. If they were to do this, then they would have better career opportunities.
3 It seems to me that people should give up smoking. If they were to do this, then they would have fewer health problems.
4 I couldn't agree more that teenagers should get a part-time job. If they were to do this, they would learn to be more responsible.
5 My opinion is that we should all do voluntary work. If we were to do this, our community would be a better place to live.

Unit 14a

10 *(Ss, in pairs do the exercise. Check Ss' answers, then individual Ss read out their sentences.)*

(Suggested answers)

2   To my mind, spending money to set up space stations is completely unjustified.
3   As far as I am concerned, in order to reduce pollution, traffic should be banned from entering the city centre.
4   I disagree that organic vegetables are much healthier than vegetables grown with chemical fertilizers.
5   It seems to me that children should be encouraged to participate in afterschool activities.

11 *(Read out the example, then Ss in pairs, give their opinion orally in class, then in writing.)*

(Suggested answers)

2   The way I see it, package holidays are ideal for people who do not like to travel alone.
3   I don't agree that becoming more aware of environmental concerns is the only way to help save our planet.
4   It seems to me that educational standards in private schools are usually higher than those in state schools.
5   In my view, boxing is an extremely violent sport and should be banned.

12 *(Explain/Elicit the meaning of any unknown words, then allow Ss three to four mins. to complete the task. Check Ss' answers.)*

a)   2 A   3 D   4 C   5 E

b)   *(Ss' own answers)*

c)   *(Elicit further points from Ss around the class. Write these on the board as notes. Then, help individual Ss to complete the task orally using the notes and their answers from parts a) and b). Ss complete the task. Ask individual Ss to read the completed extract aloud.)*

(Suggested answer)

Nowadays, we are often told what we should or should not eat. However, I personally believe that more people should stop consuming meat and become vegetarians.
   To begin with, eating meat is bad for you and has been linked to heart disease and even cancer.
   In addition, there are many healthy and tasty alternatives available. For example, soya beans and lentils are not only delicious but also good sources of protein.
   On the other hand, it can be argued that meat is an essential part of our diet and we cannot do without it. For instance, meat provides us with the protein and vitamins that we need. Moreover, vegetarian food is often boring and tasteless, since there aren't many vegetarian dishes that actually taste nice.

13 *(Allow Ss two or three mins. to skim the extracts and complete the task. Check Ss' answers, then explain/elicit the meaning of any unknown words.)*

1 = beginning   A/B   3 = ending   C
2 = ending   A   4 = beginning   B

14 *(Check that Ss understand the rubric, then allow them two or three mins. to complete the task. Check Ss' answers.)*

Key words: Fast food is a good alternative to cooking for yourself – teacher – essay expressing your opinion – giving reasons

1   B
2   A, C
3   Informal style is not suitable for this essay.

15 *(Explain/Elicit the meaning of any unknown words, then complete tasks a) and b) with the class. Ss then use the notes to talk about the topic.)*

a)   A 4, 5   B 1, 3   C 2, 6

b)   viewpoints that agree: A
     viewpoints that disagree: B, C

c)   *(Ss' own answers)*

16 *(Help individual Ss to complete the task orally in class. When satisfied that Ss can deal with the task successfully, assign it as written HW.)*

(Suggested answer)

   Nowadays, fast food has widely replaced traditional eating habits. In my opinion, although it may be an easy alternative to cooking, it can never be a really good one.
   To begin with, fast food is very unhealthy. For example, it is extremely high in fat and salt and it is not fresh. Moreover, many of the ingredients used in fast food are genetically modified.

Furthermore, fast food is expensive for both the consumer and the environment. Money spent on fast food for a week is enough to buy groceries for at least two weeks. In addition to this, fast food packaging is non-biodegradable and therefore it damages the environment.

On the other hand, it can be argued that fast food is an easy solution for people with busy lives. For instance, ordering fast food saves time and energy. People who work long hours can simply pick up the phone and order a takeaway.

All things considered, it seems to me that fast food cannot be a suitable substitute for cooking for yourself. Perhaps we should reconsider our eating habits, especially if "we are what we eat."

Unit 14b - Providing Solutions to Problems (pp. 94-97)

1 *(Allow Ss two to three mins. to look at the pictures and prepare their answers, then ask individual Ss to answer the questions orally.)*

a) 1   picture B
   2   picture C
   3   picture A

b) *(Ss' own answer)*

c) **(Suggested answers)**
   air pollution: move factories out of city; put filters in chimneys, etc.
   heavy traffic: encourage people to use public transport; ban cars from city centre, etc.
   rubbish: provide more litter bins; encourage people to recycle things, etc.

2 *(Present the theory and the paragraph plan, then read the rubric and questions aloud. Explain/Elicit the meaning of any unknown words. Help Ss to identify the key words, then Ss complete the tasks. Check Ss' answers.)*

Key words: local newspaper – articles entitled, "How can we make our city a better place to live?" – article – suggesting ways to improve city

1   Readers of the local newspaper.

2   1 b   3 e   5 a
    2 c   4 d

(Ss' own answers)

3   1 c   3 b   5 e
    2 a   4 d

(Suggested answers)
- If factories were moved out of the city, the air would no longer be dangerous to breathe.
- We should build more parks and playgrounds. If we did this, children would have somewhere safe to play.
- If wider pavements were built, people would be able to move around more easily.

3 a) *(Allow Ss two or three mins. to skim the article and label the paragraphs. Check Ss' answers.)*

Para 1:   state the problem
Para 2:   first suggestion and results/ consequences
Para 3:   second suggestion and results/ consequences
Para 4:   third suggestion and results/ consequences
Para 5:   summarise your opinion

b) *(Allow Ss four or five mins. to read the article again and prepare their answers. Discuss the answers with the class.)*

1   Formal style because it is for a newspaper.
    (Suggested answer)
    linking words/phrases, long, complex, sentences, passive voice, etc.

2   Para 2: **Suggestion:**
    - encourage people to use public transport instead of their cars especially when commuting to works
    Results: fewer cars on the road, fewer traffic jams.
    Para 3: **Suggestion:**
    - factories should be moved out of the city
    Results: the air would not be so polluted
    Para 4: **Suggestion:**
    - put more litter bins in the streets.
    Results: people would stop dropping their rubbish on the ground, our city would be cleaner.

Unit 14b

3
- First of all, it would be a good idea to...
- Furthermore...
- Secondly, steps should be taken in order to solve...
- The situation could be improved if...
- What is more, ...
- Finally, efforts should be made to...
- A useful suggestion would be to...

4
- A rhetorical question
  (Suggested answer)
  A quotation

4 *(Read out the table on useful vocabulary. Then, allow Ss three or four mins. to complete the task. Check Ss' answers, then explain/elicit the meaning of any unknown words.)*

1 **The result of this**
2 **due to the fact**
3 **it is certain that**
4 **so that**
5 **in order to**

5 a) *(Explain/Elicit the meaning of any unknown words, then complete the task with the class.)*

1 C   3 A
2 D   4 B

b) *(Individual Ss make sentences orally. Ss then repeat the task as a written exercise. Point out that Ss should use phrases from the Useful Vocabulary table on p. 95 in the Student's book.)*

(Suggested answers)
- It would be a good idea to study with a friend. Then, you could discuss any difficulties that come up.
- Another solution would be to eat properly and get enough sleep. By doing this, you would be healthy and able to concentrate.
- It would also help if you made a study plan. The result would be that your work would be more organised.

6 *(Allow Ss four mins. to complete the task. Ss work in pairs. Check Ss' answers while individual Ss read out the completed paragraphs.)*

1 C   2 A   3 B   4 D

7 *(Explain the task, then allow Ss three mins. to complete the task. Refer Ss to the useful Vocabulary table on p. 95 in the Student's Book and invite them to use phrases from there while they expand the prompts. Ss, in pairs, do the exercise. Check Ss' answers.)*

A ... In addition, you should install an alarm system. What is more, you should avoid making your house look glamorous.
B Working out three times a week would definitely help you to lose weight and keep fit. Moreover, you should follow a healthy diet and stop eating junk food.
C For instance, we should use environmentally friendly products to help reduce water pollution. In addition to this, we should plant more trees so that there will be more oxygen and fewer floods.
D It would also be a good idea to put up signs to inform the public that if they litter they will be fined. Another solution would be to organise clean-up days once a week.

8 *(Explain/Elicit the meaning of any unknown vocabulary and help Ss to identify the key words, then elicit suitable answers to the questions.)*

Key words: educational magazine – articles – discussing violence on TV – ways to stop this having negative effects on young people

1 (Ss' own answer)
2 B, D
3 1 D, 2 B
4 In the first paragraph

(Suggested answer)
A useful suggestion would be...
Another solution...
It would be a good idea if/to... etc.
In the final paragraph.

9 *(Help Ss to compose their article orally using their answers from Ex. 8. When satisfied that Ss can deal with the task successfully, assign it as written homework.)*

(Suggested answers)
Nowadays, whenever we turn on the television, we see images of cruelty and violence. The effect these images have on our children is, without a doubt, negative.

49

Unit 14c

Fortunately, however, there are certain measures that can be taken in order to deal with this problem. To begin with, the situation could be improved it we all complained to our local TV stations about the unacceptable programmes and the hours that they are shown. In this way, the stations could be convinced to air certain programmes only late at night.

Secondly, it would be a good idea to look at the TV guide and choose programmes which are suitable for children. By doing this, you could make sure your children would watch only educational and non-violent programmes.

To sum up, there are many steps that we can take to ensure that violence on TV does not have a negative influence on young people. After all, are we not all responsible for our children's well-being?

Unit 14c - Letters to the Editor (pp. 98 - 101)

1 *(Read out questions a to c and elicit suitable answers from Ss.)*

a) *(Ss' own answer)*

b) I would feel very upset.

c) I would write a letter to the editor of a local newspaper.

2 *(Present the theory and the theory plan. Read the rubric and help Ss underline the key words, then Ss answer questions 1 to 4.)*

Key words: local council — town you live in — build large shopping centre — letter to editor of local newspaper — expressing your views

1 The editor of the local newspaper.

2 To express your views on the local council's decision to build a large shopping centre.

3 I would begin my letter with **Dear Sir/Madam**, and I would end my letter with **Yours faithfully + my full name** because I do not know the editor of the local newspaper.

4 a) **(Suggested answer)**
   Yes. You can buy many things at the shopping centre in my town i.e. clothes, jewellery, books, shoes, etc. It is very popular with shoppers.

b) noise pollution, heavy traffic litter in the streets ✓

c) **(Suggested answer)**
No.
The advantages of having a shopping centre near my house would be that there would be a variety of shops close to my home so it would be very convenient.
The disadvantages of having a shopping centre near my house would be that the streets would be crowded, there would be a lot of noise pollution and air pollution due to heavy traffic, and many of the smaller shops in my town would close down.

3 *(Allow Ss three mins. to skim the letter and label the paragraphs. Check Ss' answers.)*

a) Para 1: reason for writing and opinion
   Para 2: first problem and consequences
   Para 3: second problem and consequences
   Para 4: summary of opinion

b) The writer disagrees with the local council's decision.

4 *(Allow Ss two mins. to skim the letter and complete the table. Ss, then, make sentences. Check Ss' answers.)*

Problems	Consequences
• increase in amount of traffic and number of people	suffer from air and noise pollution
• oldest and most beautiful buildings torn down	Trent's surroundings and character destroyed

In order for the shopping centre to be built, some of our oldest and most beautiful buildings will have to be torn down. Therefore, Trent's surroundings as well as its character will be destroyed.

5 *(Read out the table of Useful expressions and linking words/phrases. Ss, then do Ex. 5.)*

I believe   = I think/feel, etc
Firstly   = First of all
Obviously   = Clearly

As a result = This would mean/Consequently, etc
Secondly = What is more/Furthermore, etc
Therefore = Then/Consequently/If we did this, etc
I am totally opposed to = I strongly disagree with
I believe = I think/feel, etc
Consequently = As a result
I hope that the council will (reconsider its decision) = I hope my comments will be taken into consideration/ I hope something will be done about this urgently, etc

6 *(Read out the examples, then Ss do the exercise orally in class. Assign it as written HW.)*

3 I am (totally) opposed to the construction of a new motorway.
4 Furthermore, the council should provide more sports centres.
5 I am writing to express my disapproval of plans to close The Majestic Cinema.
6 I feel that cars should be banned from the city centre.
7 I think that more policemen should patrol our neighbourhood.
8 I believe the new library is an excellent idea.
9 I hope my comments will be taken into consideration.

7 *(Allow Ss three mins. to complete the task. Check Ss' answers.)*

1 B   2 A

a **Letter 1:** He/She is writing to express his/her disagreement with a letter about cyclists he/she has read in a magazine.
Letter 2: He/She is writing to express his/her approval of the recycling plant to be built in his/ her town.

b The writer disagrees with the article he/she read in the magazine about cyclists. The writer agrees with the council's decision to build a recycling plant.

8 2 F → I think that all shops should be open from 10 am to 9 pm during the week. This would mean that working people will not be restricted as to when to do their shopping.
3 A → In my opinion, pedestrians should always use zebra crossings. By doing this, they would avoid the risk of being hit by motorists.

4 B → I am totally in favour of all blocks of flats having security guards. In this way, tenants would be protected on a 24-hour basis.
5 D → I strongly agree with the airport being built 20 km away from the city centre. Consequently, residents will not be affected by air traffic.
6 E → I feel that the newspaper should have a weekly supplement on cultural happenings in town. Then, people would be better informed and they would have the opportunity to book tickets in advance.

9 *(Help Ss underline the key words in the rubric, then answer the questions.)*

a) **Key words:** news report – *Rosemary Telegraph* – write letter to editor – making suggestions – how to make park more appealing

1 The editor of the *Rosemary Telegraph*.
2 The reason for writing my letter is to make suggestions on how to make the park more appealing.
3 I would begin my letter with **Dear Sir** and I would end my letter with **Yours faithfully + my full name**.

b) 2 C → A: Do you think the park should have drinking fountains?
B: Yes, I do. Then, we could have a drink whenever we are thirsty.
3 F → A: Do you think the park should have swings, sandboxes and so on?
B: Yes, I do. Then, our children would be able to play safely and have fun.
4 A → A: Do you think the park should have picnic tables?
B: Yes, I do. Then, we could bring our own food and have a picnic.
5 B → A: Do you think the park should have public lavatories?
B: Yes, I do. Then, we would be able to wash our hands, change babies' nappies and so on.
6 E → A: Do you think the park should have rubbish bins?
B: Yes, I do. Then, we wouldn't drop rubbish on the ground.

c) *(Ss' own answers)*

Unit 15

10 *(When satisfied that Ss can deal with the task successfully, assign it as written HW.)*

(Suggested answer)
Dear Sir/Madam,
    I am writing to express my approval of the local council's decision to improve Rosemary Park and I would like to make some suggestions.
    Firstly, I believe that drinking fountains should be installed so that visitors to the park could have a drink whenever they were thirsty.
    It would also be a good idea to have a snack bar in the park, to enable people to buy a cool drink and have something light to eat.
    Secondly, I think that the park should have more rubbish bins. This would help to keep the park clean, since visitors would not drop rubbish on the ground.
    What is more, Rosemary Park should have public lavatories. This would allow people to wash their hands, use the toilets, change babies' nappies and so on.
    To sum up, it is my opinion that the local council's decision to spend more money on the improvement of Rosemary Park is an extremely wise one. I hope my suggestions will be taken into consideration.
    Yours faithfully,
    Jane Williams

Unit 15 - Assessment and Proposal Reports (pp. 102 - 107)

1 *(Explain the meaning of **questionnaire**, then read the items aloud. Explain/Elicit the meaning of any unknown words. Ss then listen and tick the correct boxes. Check Ss' answers. Ss listen again and complete the comments. Check Ss' answers, then ask individual Ss to give a brief oral report to the class.)*

	Excellent ****	Good ***	Average **	Poor *
Location only an hour from **London**, nearest station twenty minutes away			✓	
Facilities **tennis** courts, beautiful large bedrooms, a swimming **pool**		✓		
Treatments many on offer, **huge** choice, all wonderful	✓			
Food rather **boring** and tasteless, but low in fat and very **healthy**			✓	
General Comments Oaklands' facilities very **good;** an excellent **range** of treatments available; food rather **disappointing** — the menu could be improved				

2 *(Present the theory and the paragraph plan. Read the rubric and the questions aloud and help Ss to identify the key words. Allow Ss two or three mins. to answer the questions. Check Ss' answers.)*

Key words: assistant manager – international publishing company – tourist guide to restaurants in your country – the manager – assess a restaurant in your area – report – describing food, service, prices and atmosphere

  1 The aim is to assess the suitability of a restaurant; therefore, I should write an assessment report.
  2 The manager of the company I work for.
  3 B
  4 Tourists who do not have a lot of money to spend.
  5 C, D, E, F, H

6 Formal style. Formal style is factual and impersonal and it uses full verb forms, passive voice, formal linking words/phrases/idioms, etc.

7 a (Ss' own answers)
  b **(Suggested answer)**
  Some dishes are quite expensive.
  The prices are reasonable.
  The atmosphere is very relaxing.
  The salads are disgusting.
  The restaurant is rather noisy.
  The service is extremely slow/efficient.

3 a) *(Allow Ss five mins. to read the text and fill in the headings. Check Ss' answers, then explain/elicit the meaning of any words which Ss still do not understand. Individual Ss read aloud from the report.)*

1 as well as	4 However
2 also	5 and
3 Despite	6 Even though
A Introduction	D Prices
B Food	E Atmosphere
C Service	F Recommendation

b) *(Allow Ss three or four mins. to read the text again and complete the table. Check Ss' answers.)*

Subheadings	Positive Points	Negative Points
Food	good quality meals, wide variety of delicious local and international dishes, excellent choice of starters and desserts, number of French specialities	
Service	staff well-trained, polite	sometimes slow, problem when the restaurant is full
Prices	quite reasonable	some dishes, (e.g. French specialities) are rather expensive
Atmosphere	charming and relaxing, background music pleasant, soft lighting creates cosy atmosphere, modern decor, appeals to customers of all ages	

(Suggested answer)

Gaslights serves good quality meals. It has a wide variety of delicious local and international dishes. The service can sometimes be a bit slow, but the staff are well-trained and polite. The prices are quite reasonable, although some dishes, such as the French specialities, are rather expensive. The atmosphere is charming and relaxing, the background music is pleasant and the decor is modern. Gaslights Restaurant appeals to customers of all ages.

c) *(Ss' own answers)*

4 a) *(Allow Ss five or six mins. to read the sentences and insert the linking words/phrases. Check Ss' answers, then explain/elicit the meaning of any words which Ss still do not understand. Individual Ss read aloud from the report.)*

2 therefore
3 Although, as
4 In addition, On the other hand
5 and, Alternatively

b) *(Allow Ss two or three mins. to read the sentences again and complete the task. Check Ss' answers.)*

C 5   D 1   F 3   G 4

(Read out the Useful Expressions box, then ask Ss to skim the report in Ex. 3 and find which expressions the writer has used to start and end his report, then suggest alternatives.)

5 *(Read the rubric and the questions aloud and help Ss to identify the key words. Allow Ss two or three mins. to answer the questions. Check Ss' answers.)*

Key words: you work for – company – planning to hold – annual winter excursion – manager – write – report – suitability – Mountain High Hotel – information about rooms – facilities – food and cost – commenting on hotel's good and bad points

1 To assess the suitability of the Mountain High Hotel for the company's annual winter excursion. It is an assessment report.
2 The manager of the company I work for.

6 a) *(Allow Ss four mins. to complete the task, in pairs. Check Ss' answers.)*

Rooms:
- private bathroom in each room
- comfortable rooms with colour TV
- no telephones in rooms
- no room service

Facilities:
- cosy lounge with fireplace
- live music every weekend
- free skiing lessons
- three-star restaurant
- guests can rent skiing equipment

Food:
- limited choice of dishes for vegetarians
- delicious home-made meals
- varied menu

Cost:
- breakfast not included in price
- £60 double room, £45 single room
- no special rates for groups with fewer than thirty people

b) **positive points:**
- private bathroom in each room
- £60 double room, £45 single room
- comfortable rooms with colour TV
- cosy lounge with fireplace
- live music every weekend
- free skiing lessons
- three-star restaurant
- guests can rent skiing equipment
- delicious home-made meals
- varied menu

Negative points:
- breakfast not included in price
- limited choice of dishes for vegetarians
- no special rates for groups with fewer than thirty people
- no telephones in rooms
- no room service

c) (See Ex. 7 – Suggested answer – Introduction)

d) (See Ex. 7 – Suggested answer – Recommendation)

7 (Refer Ss to the plan on p102. Elicit suitable points to be included in the introduction and conclusion and write these on the board in note form. Help Ss to complete the report orally using the notes and their answers from Ex. 6. When satisfied that Ss can deal with the task successfully, assign it as written homework.)

(Suggested answer)

To: Jack Brown, Manager
From: Michelle Smith, Assistant Manager
Subj.: Mountain High Hotel
Date: 6th November, 20...

Introduction
The purpose of this report is to assess the suitability of the Mountain High Hotel for the company's annual winter excursion.

Rooms
All rooms are comfortable and have private bathrooms and colour televisions. However, there are no telephones and room service is not available.

Facilities
The hotel has a cosy lounge with a fireplace and there is live music every weekend. In addition to this, the hotel rents skiing equipment to guests and provides free lessons to beginners. Moreover, there is a three-star restaurant which serves delicious home-made meals. Although the menu is varied, there is a limited choice for vegetarians.

Cost
A single room costs £45 and a double costs £60. Special rates are offered, but only to groups of more than thirty people. What is more, breakfast is not included in the price.

Recommendation
To sum up, even though there is no room service, no telephones in the rooms and few vegetarian dishes, the hotel's facilities satisfy our requirements and the prices are reasonable. Therefore, it is my opinion that Mountain High Hotel be recommended for the company's annual winter excursion.

8 (Allow Ss two or three mins. to complete the task. Check Ss' answers.)

1 T	4 T	7 T	9 T
2 T	5 F	8 F	10 T
3 F	6 T		

9 (Allow Ss three or four mins. to read the extracts and complete the task. Then explain/elicit the meaning of any vocabulary which Ss still do not understand. Check Ss' answers.)

A 1 For example ...   4 fashionable ...
   2 therefore ...   5 Finally ...
   3 What is more ...   6 excellent

B 1 The aim of this report is ...
   2 increase the number of ...

C 1 To sum up ...   3 special
   2 attract   4 offered

10 *(Present the theory, then read the rubric and the questions aloud. Help Ss to identify the key words, then Ss complete the task. Check Ss' answers.)*

Key words: part-time job – bookshop – educational publications – manager – attract young customers – report – making suggestions

1 To suggest ways to make the bookshop more attractive to young customers.
2 A proposal report.
3 The manager of the bookshop.
4 A, C, D, E and F
5 Formal style → factual language, passive voice full verb forms, formal linking words, advanced vocabulary, etc.

11 a) *(Check that Ss understand the meaning of the subheadings, then allow Ss four or five mins. to read the report and complete the task. Check Ss' answers, then explain/elicit the meaning of any words that Ss still do not understand.)*

A Purpose
B Types of Books
C Other items on Sale
D Discounts
E Shop Interior
F Conclusion

b) *(Elicit suitable oral answers to the questions.)*

1 In paragraphs 2, 3, 4 and 5
   Para 2 – offer magazines and books on topics such as music, fashion and computers

   Para 3 – stock items designed for young people, such as school equipment, posters, stickers, school bags and games

   Para 4 – discounts would encourage local students to buy their textbooks at the bookshop. Leaflets should be given to schools and colleges to make students aware of these discounts

Para 5 – decor was modernised and the interior was painted in bright colours

2 **Modals to be underlined:**
   B ... the shop <u>should</u> offer ...
   C It <u>would</u> be a good idea ...
   D Discount <u>would</u> encourage ... leaflets <u>should</u> be given ...
   E Young people <u>would</u> be ...
   F ...the bookshop <u>would</u> attract ...

3 The aim of this report is to propose measures which would attract young customers to the bookshop.

12 a) *(Read the rubric and the questions aloud. Explain/Elicit the meaning of any unknown words. Then Ss underline the key words and answer the questions. Check Ss' answers.)*

Key words: youth club — manager — make club more popular with 10- to 14-year-olds — report making suggestions

1 My manager.
2 To make suggestions about how to make the club more popular with 10- to 14-year-olds.
3 A proposal report.
4 Yes.
   (Suggested answer)
   Introduction, Opening Hours, Facilities, Decor, Publicity, Recommendation
5 In paragraphs 2, 3, 4 and 5

b) *(Read the main points and suggestions aloud and explain/elicit the meaning of any unknown words. Allow Ss three or four mins. to match the items, then individual Ss form appropriate sentences orally; if desired, Ss may then repeat the task as a written exercise.)*

2 D   3 C   4 B

(Ss' own answers)

c) *(Elicit from Ss which of the subheadings are suitable, then allow Ss two mins. to match them to the points. Check Ss' answers.)*

C 4   D 1   E 3

Unit 15

55

13 *(Refer Ss to the plan on p. 102. Elicit suitable points to be included in the introduction and conclusion, and write these on the board in note form. Help Ss to complete the report orally using the notes and their answers from Ex. 12. When satisfied that Ss can deal with the task successfully, assign it as written HW.)*

(Suggested answer)
Introduction
The purpose of this report is to recommend ways to make Thorntree Youth Club more popular with 10- to 14-year-olds.

Opening Hours
To begin with, the youth club does not open until 7 pm, which is rather late for 10- to 14-year-olds. If the club opened earlier, then younger children could go there straight from school.

Facilities
At present, the youth club's facilities are more suitable for older teenagers. If other activities were organised (for example, table tennis tournaments or computer games), then this would be more fun for 10- to 14-year-olds.

Decor
The present interior of Thorntree Youth Club is not decorated in a way that appeals to younger children. If colourful posters were put up and modern furniture was bought, then this would brighten up the club and make it more appealing.

Publicity
Furthermore, the current publicity is not aimed at younger members. Leaflets could be given out at local schools so that 10- to 14-year-olds would find out about the club and perhaps want to join.

Recommendation
In conclusion, the youth club would become more popular with 10- to 14-year-olds if the opening hours were changed. What is more, attractive decor and well-publicised activities suitable for younger children would certainly attract more young people in this age group.

Revision & Extension Section (pp. 109 - 143)

1 *(Present the theory and explain/elicit the meaning of any unknown vocabulary, then read the rubric and the questions aloud. Allow Ss two or three mins. to underline the key words and answer the questions. Check Ss' answers.)*

Key words: close relative — got married — cousin — not able to come — write letter — describing wedding — whole day — preparations — ceremony — some people who attended

1 letter to a friend which includes the description of an event/celebration
2 a) B, C, E
   b) • In the main body
      • 3 paragraphs — one for each topic
3 Para 1
4 B

2 *(Allow Ss two or three mins. to skim the text and label the paragraphs. Check Ss' answers.)*

Para 1: opening remarks & reason for writing
Para 2: preparations
Para 3: actual ceremony
Para 4: people who attended
Para 5: closing remarks

(Elicit suitable answers from Ss around the class.)

1 Informal.
2 i) an informal greeting (Dear Iris,)
  ii) "chatty", personal tone (I hope you're well.)
  iii) everyday vocabulary (It's a pity)
  iv) colloquial expressions/idioms (you couldn't make it)
  v) short forms (It's, couldn't, I'd, etc)
  vi) an informal ending (Love, Jess)
3 In the introduction, the writer has included opening remarks and has stated the reason for writing.
4 Paragraph 4.
5 **descriptive adjectives to be underlined (suggested synonyms in brackets):**
wonderful (brilliant) — beautiful (pretty) — lovely (great) — stunning (gorgeous) — great (handsome) — perfect (ideal) — lovely (beautiful) — touching (moving) — funny (strange)

Revision & Extension Section

3 *(Allow Ss two or three mins. to read the introduction and conclusion again. Read the notes aloud and help Ss to complete the task orally. Ss then repeat the task in writing.)*

(Suggested answers)

How are things with you? Sorry that you couldn't make it to Kim's wedding. Let me tell you all about it.

Well, that's all for now. Please give my love to your mum and dad. Write back soon to tell me all your news.

4 *(Present the useful language, then read the rubric aloud and allow Ss two mins. to underline the key words. Read the questions aloud, then Ss complete the task. Check Ss' answers.)*

Key words: favourite magazine – competition – article – "The Perfect Pet" – giving reasons – mention how you would take care of your pet

1 B
2 B, C, D
3 B
  D
  C
4 **(Suggested answers)**
  Dog – make good companions
       – obedient
       – fun to play with
5 **(Suggested answers)**
  – the correct food
  – regular exercise
  – love and affection
  – a clean, comfortable place to live

5 *(Present the paragraph plan, then allow Ss five or six mins. to read the text and put the verbs into the correct form. Check Ss' answers around the class, then elicit suitable answers to the questions. Finally, ask individual Ss to read aloud from the completed text.)*

1 are
2 cheers
3 will respond/responds
4 will become/becomes
5 will learn/learns
6 had
7 would look after
8 had
9 would train

1 Opinion.
2 Formal – because it is an article giving an opinion and the reader is unknown to us.
3 General remarks introducing the topic and stating your opinion.

4 A well-known saying has been included. *(man's best friend)*
5 A dog.
6 Dogs are good companions; dogs feel affection and like to please their owners; dogs can be useful.
7 Paragraphs 2 - 4.
8 You should feed it the right food at the right time, and exercise it regularly. You must take it to the vet for regular check-ups, train it and love it.
9 Yes, the main points are included in clear topic sentences.

Topic sentences to be underlined:
– To start with, dogs make perfect pets because they are good companions.
– In addition, dogs make the most loyal pets because they feel great affection for their owners and like to please them.
– What is more, dogs can be very useful.
– If I had a dog, I would look after it by feeding it the right food at the right time and making sure it had plenty of exercise.

10 *(Help Ss to identify the linking words/phrases in the paragraphs. Write these on the board, then elicit which category they belong to.)*

Para 2: To start with, because, For example, and, then
Para 3: In addition, because, and, because
Para 4: What is more, For instance, or, For this reason
Para 5: and, and, because

A – **list points:** To start with, and, In addition, What is more, or
B – **explain reasons/results:** because, then, For this reason
C – **introduce examples:** For example, For instance

11 *(Allow Ss three mins. to read the article again. Ask Ss around the class to suggest alternative linking words.)*

(Suggested answers)

In the first place, furthermore, moreover, secondly, besides, therefore, so, etc

6 *(Read the notes aloud. Allow Ss two mins. to match the viewpoints and reasons/examples, then help Ss to complete the task orally. Ss then repeat the task in writing. Check Ss' answers by asking individual Ss to read their paragraphs aloud.)*

1 C   2 D   3 B   4 A

57

Revision & Extension Section

(Suggested answer)

To begin with, goldfish make ideal pets because they are easy to look after. For example, you only need to feed them a pinch of food once a day. Also, they don't make the house untidy, because, unlike dogs and cats, they don't make a mess. In addition, goldfish are not expensive to look after, since their food costs very little and they do not have to be taken to the vet. Finally, goldfish make ideal pets because they can help you relax. For instance, research has shown that watching fish can actually reduce stress.

7 **a)** *(Present the theory, then read the extracts aloud. Ss match them to the styles. Check Ss' answers.)*

    A 3   B 2   C 1

b) *(Allow Ss two mins. to read the extracts again and complete the task. Check Ss' answers.)*

    A 3   B 1   C 2

c) *(Read the prompts aloud, then help Ss to complete the task orally. Ss then repeat the task in writing. Check Ss' answers by asking individual Ss to read their introduction aloud.)*

(Suggested answer)

What makes a good pen friend? Everyone has a different answer to this question, but there are some qualities which we all look for in a pen friend.

8 *(Read the rubric and the questions aloud. Allow Ss three or four mins. to underline the key words and complete the task.)*

Key words: "Everybody can do something to help reduce crime in their neighbourhood" – composition – whether or not agree – suggestions about how crime can be prevented

1 *(Ss' own answers)*
2 **(Suggested answers)**

    It would be a good idea to ...
    The best thing would be to ...
    One solution would be to ...
    One way to ...

9 *(Present the paragraph plan, then allow Ss four or five mins. to read the article and replace the words in bold. Check Ss' answers, then ask individual Ss to read aloud from the corrected text.)*

1 serious problem
2 members of the local community
3 more difficult
4 Parents
5 children
6 Needless to say
7 reduce

(Elicit suitable answers from Ss around the class.)

1 Yes, the introduction clearly states the topic.
2 The writer agrees with the statement. *(I agree that everyone can play a part in helping to reduce it.)*
3 The writer asks a rhetorical question.
4 Start with a quotation/address the reader directly.

(Suggested answer)

If you speak to your friends and neighbours, it is almost certain that one of them has been a victim of crime. Crime is on the increase and I agree that everyone can work together to reduce it.

5 **Expressions to be underlined:**
   – One way to prevent crime would be
   – Another solution would be
   – we could
   – It would also be a good idea

6 **Results**
   – fewer crimes would be committed
   – it wouldn't be so easy for criminals to break in and steal things
   – it would cut down on the number of crimes committed by children

7 **(Suggested answer)**

In my opinion, we all have a responsibility to reduce crime in our society, for the sake of future generations. It is up to us to make the world a safer place to live in.

10 **a)** *(Read the rubric aloud and allow Ss two or three mins. to underline the key words and answer the questions.)*

Key words: teacher – composition – "Everyone can help to make our roads safer" – agree or disagree – suggestions about how road safety can be improved – explaining reasons

1 semi-formal
2 A, C, D

b) *(Elicit whether Ss around the class agree or disagree, then allow Ss two or three mins. to match the points. Elicit which points support Ss' views, then ask Ss to make appropriate sentences. Check Ss' answers.)*

Revision & Extension Section

1 A 2 E 3 C 4 D 5 B

(Ss' own answers)

11 *(Present the paragraph plan. Then, help Ss to complete the task orally using their answers from Ex. 10. When satisfied that Ss can deal with the task successfully, assign it as written HW.)*

(Suggested answer)

How many times have you seen a terrible car crash on the news or in the paper? The number of road accidents seems to be increasing all the time, and I certainly agree that everyone can do something to help make our roads safer.

To begin with, the government should introduce stricter penalties for drivers who break the law. Heavy fines, for instance, would make people think twice before speeding.

In addition, people could use their cars less or share with others going in the same direction. If they did this, there would be fewer cars on the road, which would mean that there would be fewer accidents.

Finally, even pedestrians and cyclists can help to make the roads safer. To avoid being involved in accidents, people should take more care when crossing roads, and cyclists should be more alert when riding in traffic.

In conclusion, everyone uses our roads, so it is everyone's responsibility to improve road safety in any way they can.

12 *(Read the rubric and questions aloud. Allow Ss two or three mins. to underline the key words and answer the questions. Check Ss' answers.)*

Key words: local newspaper – sports centre or entertainment centre – opinion – article – which should be built – give reasons – what you would like the centre to offer

1 An opinion essay.
2 **(Suggested answer)**
The town has very few facilities for entertainment. There is already a modern sports centre in the town. The centre should have a cinema, a theatre, a coffee shop, etc.

13 *(Present the paragraph plan, then allow Ss four or five mins to read the model and answer the questions. Check Ss' answers.)*

1 **(Suggested answer)**
Does Blakely need another sports centre?
2 Formal - because it is an opinion article written for an unknown reader.
3 A new entertainment centre, because there are already enough sports facilities in the town, but few for entertainment.
4 Theatre, cinema, disco, exhibition hall, coffee shop, restaurant
5 Present simple and present perfect passive.
6 In addition to = Apart from (Para 2)
On the other hand = However (Para 3)
Furthermore = Moreover (Para 4)
In conclusion = To sum up (Para 5)
7 **(Suggested introduction)**
As you all probably know, Blakely has recently been given a sum of money to be spent on either a sports centre or an entertainment centre. In my opinion, we need more entertainment facilities.

(Suggested conclusion)
All in all, I feel that there is no contest. Blakely is already so well served by sports facilities that the choice is obvious – the money would certainly be better spent on an entertainment centre.

14 *(Read the rubric and questions aloud. Allow Ss two or three mins. to underline the key words and answer the questions.)*

Key words: international magazine – articles – Influential People of the Twentieth Century – short article – a person influential in your country during the twentieth century

1 An article about a person.
2 No - because the title states that you must write about people from the twentieth century.
3 (Ss' own answers)
4 physical appearance, character, interests, historical importance, in what way influential

15 *(Present the paragraph plan, then allow Ss four or five mins. to read the model and answer the questions. Check Ss' answers.)*
1 It has been written in formal style.
• formal expressions/phrases (*on the contrary, in addition, furthermore*)
• advanced vocabulary (*positive influence, harassed*)
• passive voice (*was harassed, was not discouraged, was devoted*)

59

Revision & Extension Section

2   name of person, comment about their influence
    (Suggested answer)
    Throughout the twentieth century there were many people who were influential in different ways. Undoubtedly, the one who had the most positive and lasting influence was Diana, Princess of Wales.
3   To describe the influence the person had.
    Topic sentence:
    Diana was a great influence on the country for many reasons.
4   She helped many people, helped to change negative attitudes towards illnesses, taught others to be kind and considerate and helpful.
5   organised charity events – made public more aware of the problems of the less fortunate – set an example
6   **Linking words used to list points/give examples:** and – also – In addition – not only ... but also – First – such as – Furthermore – for example
    Linking words to show contrast:
    Nevertheless – On the contrary

16 *(Read the rubric and questions aloud. Allow Ss two or three mins. to underline the key words and answer the questions.)*

Key words: international magazine – articles – friends and friendship – what you think makes an ideal friendship

1   An opinion essay.
2   **(Suggested answer)**
    trust, honesty, loyalty, having similar interests and opinions, being dependable

17 *(Present the paragraph plan, then allow Ss four or five mins. to read the model and answer the questions. Check Ss' answers.)*

1   **(Suggested answer)** "The Perfect Friend".
2   Semi-formal.
3   i) semi-formal style (*A proper friendship is one based on equality*)
    ii) few short forms (*I believe it is ...*)
    iii) use of linking words/expressions (*Firstly, Secondly, Thirdly*)
    iv) addressing the reader directly (*What does the word friendship mean to you?*)
4   Yes, the introduction clearly states the topic (*What does the word friendship mean to you ... The ideal friendship is much more than that.*)
5   **Techniques:**
    – addressing the reader directly
    – **(Suggested answer)**
    What is the perfect friendship and does it actually exist? Everyone has relationships with other people, but only some can be described as friendship. True friendship is sometimes difficult to find, because it demands such commitment from everyone involved.
6   • trust and honesty
    • similar interests
    • support in times of trouble
    Yes, each point has been presented in a separate paragraph with a clear topic sentence.
    Topic sentences to be underlined:
    Firstly, a true friend should be honest and trustworthy.
    Secondly, I believe it is important to share similar interests with your friend.
    Thirdly, an ideal friend is one you can turn to in times of trouble.
7   **Words used to list points (alternatives in brackets):** Firstly (To begin with) – Secondly (Additionally) – Thirdly (Finally)
8   Para 2 – point: a true friend should be honest and trustworthy.
             reason: without these characteristics, you cannot have a good relationship with anyone.
    Para 3 – point: it is important to share similar interests with your friend.
             reason: it would be very difficult to keep a friendship going if the two people had nothing in common.
    Para 4 – point: an ideal friend is one who you can turn to in times of trouble.
             reason: friendship is not only about having a good time, but being able to give or ask for support whenever it is needed.
9   The writer ends the article by summarising the points covered in the main body.

18 *(Read the rubric and questions aloud. Allow Ss two or three mins. to underline the key words and answer the questions. Check Ss' answers.)*

Key words: Only people who know how to make music can really enjoy listening to it – teacher – write a composition – your views

Revision & Extension Section

1 An opinion essay.
2 (Ss' own answers)
3 (Ss' own answers)

19 *(Present the paragraph plan, then allow Ss four or five mins. to read the model and answer the questions. Check Ss' answers.)*

1 The writer disagrees with the topic.
   (I strongly believe that the ability to enjoy music does <u>not</u> depend on the ability to make music.)
2 The writer begins with a rhetorical question in the introduction and addresses the reader directly.
   (Suggested answer)
   Some people believe that you cannot enjoy music unless you play a musical instrument or sing. I disagree with this, since I enjoy listening to music but do not actually play any instruments myself.
3 Yes, the writer has presented arguments both for and against the statement.
   Para 2 – (against) not having musical talent doesn't stop you from enjoying music
   Para 3 – (against) anyone is capable of enjoying music because it relates to emotions, not education, knowledge or ability
   Para 4 – (for) knowledge of music can help understanding music more clearly and appreciating it
4 The topic sentences in Paras 2, 3 and 4 (1st sentence of each paragraph) clearly state the writer's arguments.
   Justifications
   Para 2 – personal experience
   Para 3 – babies and animals react positively to music
   Para 4 – understanding music makes you able to appreciate it
5 **Linking words/expressions used to list points (alternatives in brackets):** To begin with (Firstly) – Although (Despite the fact that) – Furthermore (Moreover) – On the other hand (Alternatively) – To sum up (In conclusion)
6 **(Suggested answer)**
   In conclusion, although having musical ability can lead to a greater understanding and appreciation of music, this does not necessarily mean that you cannot listen to and enjoy different types of music.

20 *(Read the rubric and questions aloud. Allow Ss two or three mins. to underline the key words and answer the questions. Check Ss' answers.)*

Key words: friend – improve his/her English – letter in reply – giving advice – the main difficulties

1 A letter giving advice.
2 **(Suggested answer)**
   You could enrol in a class at a college or university.
   You should try to make friends with a native speaker of English.

21 *(Present the paragraph plan, then allow Ss about five mins. to read the letter and answer the questions. Check Ss answers around the class.)*

1 Informal – because it is written to a friend.
2 i) informal greeting/ending (*Dear Juan, Regards, Maya*)
   ii) informal introduction (*Thanks for your last letter.*)
   iii) idiom (*practice makes perfect*)
   iv) short forms (*it's, I'd, you'll, etc.*)
3 To give advice.
   (*... I'd be happy to give you any advice I can.*)
4 Para 2 – start a course in English
   Para 3 – make friends with someone who is a native English speaker
   Para 4 – read magazines or books, watch films and TV programmes in English
5 The best thing you can do ... – If I were you ... – It would also be a good idea.
   (Suggested answers)
   – It might help if you ...
   – You would do well to ...
   – Why don't you try ...
6 – qualified teachers will be able to teach you properly
   – be able to practise what you learn in class
   – gives you a lot of useful practice, and it's fun at the same time
7 To name difficulties Juan might encounter.
   (*Of course, you will have a few problems, ...*)
8 **(Suggested answer)**
   Write soon to let me know how your English is improving. I'm sure your studies will go better than you expect!

22 *(Allow Ss three or four mins. to read the rubric and answer the questions. Check Ss' answers around the class.)*

61

Revision & Extension Section

1 A letter giving advice
2 **(Suggested answers)**
Make sure you know which material will be tested.
Set aside adequate time for studying.

23 a) *(Allow Ss three to four mins. to read the notes and reasons and match the items. Check Ss' answers and elicit appropriate sentences. The task can then be assigned as written homework.)*

2 D   3 A   4 E   5 B

(Suggested answers)
2 You should get plenty of sleep. You can't learn properly if you're tired.
3 It would be a good idea to revise questions in past tests or exams. This way you'll be able to practise answering exam questions.
4 Why don't you use coloured pens to highlight important points? This way it'll be easy to find the key points in your notes, and you'll remember these more easily.
5 You'd better not try to study every book in the library as there is a limit to how much information you can learn.

b) *(Ss' own answers)*

24 *(Allow Ss three mins. to read the rubric again and refer them back to the paragraph plan on p. 122. Discuss the task, and when you are sure Ss understand the instructions, assign as homework.)*

(Suggested answer)
Dear Stephanie,
   It sounds as if things are going well for you at university. I can understand how nervous you are about your first exams, and I am happy to provide you with some study tips that helped me during my first year.
   The most important thing to remember is not to wait until the last minute to study. You might want to consider making a study timetable, setting aside some time each evening to study specific topics. If you do this, you will avoid exhaustion and panic right before your exam.
   Also, if I were you, I would buy some coloured highlighters. If you highlight important points as you come across them, you will automatically have a study guide to use before your exams.

   Remember, people sometimes panic just before an exam. This is natural, but there are things you can do to avoid this. Be sure to get a good night's rest before your exam and to eat a good breakfast in the morning so you will feel your best. Allow plenty of time to get to your exam, so you won't feel rushed.
   Exam time can be difficult, especially when all your tests fall during the same week. I can tell you from experience that being prepared and organised is the best way to avoid problems.
   I hope some of this advice helps. You have always been a good student and I know nothing has changed now that you are at university! Say hello to your family for me, and let me know how you did as soon as you get your results.

   Lots of love,
   Ralph

25 *(Allow Ss two or three mins. to read the rubric and underline the key words, then answer the questions. Check Ss' answers.)*

Key words: travel magazine – short story competition – excursion to remember – must begin – As soon as Bob arrived in the city, he knew that this would be a wonderful day

1 Yes, because the story begins
   As soon as Bob arrived in the city ...
2 *(Ss' own answers)*
3 Third person, because the story begins
   As soon as **Bob** *...*

26 *(Present the paragraph plan, then allow Ss six or seven mins. to read the model and answer the questions. Check Ss' answers.)*

1 the people involved – Bob, his brother, (chauffeur)
   time – the morning
   place – in the city, London, station
   weather – the morning sun was bright
   feelings – Bob and his brother were excited, Bob smiled to himself, felt very important
2 The main body consists of 3 paragraphs:
   Para 2 – sightseeing
   Para 3 – lunch at a famous restaurant
   Para 4 – the performance
3 • **Past simple** is the most commonly used tense because the story describes something that has already taken place.

- **Past perfect:** to relate events which happened before another action in the past.
- **Past continuous:** to set the scene/to describe events that were in progress in the past.

4 big – huge; looking – staring; said – whispered

5 **Words/Expressions to be underlined (alternatives in brackets):** As soon as (The minute that), The first place they visited (First of all they visited), Then (Next), The next thing (Afterwards)

6 **Words/Expressions to be circled (alternatives in brackets):** excited (thrilled), amazed (stunned), marvelled (gazed in wonder), fantastic (magical), exhausted (tired)

7 limousine – shiny, black
buildings – huge, beautiful
restaurant – famous, expensive
performance – incredible

8 i The writer has used direct speech.
ii **(Other techniques)** refer to people's feelings, comments or reactions.
(Suggested answer)
As soon as they got home, Bob went straight to bed. He was tired but happy. After all, you don't win first prize every day, do you?

27 *(Read the rubric and questions aloud. Allow Ss two or three mins. to underline the key words and answer the questions. Check Ss' answers.)*

Key words: "Screen" magazine – prefer going to cinema/watching videos at home – article – which **you** prefer – give reasons

1 An opinion essay
2 (Ss' own answers)

28 *(Present the paragraph plan, then allow Ss five or six mins. to read the model and answer the questions. Check Ss' answers.)*

1 The writer prefers the cinema.
2 **(Suggested answer)**
What would you rather do on a Friday night – go to the cinema or watch a video? Since the invention of the video recorder, it is felt that the cinema has become less popular than before. However, although the video has lots of advantages, I still prefer the whole experience of going to the cinema.

3 The writer gives his opinion in Paras 2-4.
Para 2 – Firstly, ...
Para 3 – Secondly, ...
Para 4 – Furthermore, ...

4 • An evening at the cinema is an exciting outing – can meet friends, go for a meal
• Modern cinemas have excellent projectors and sound equipment – the film is more gripping, you feel part of the action
• You can see the latest releases – you don't have to wait a year for the film to come out on video

5 The opposing view is given in para 5 – Videos are cheap and convenient and you can watch them in the comfort of your own home whenever you like and as many times as you want.

6 **Tenses used:** present simple, present perfect

7 **Descriptive adjectives (alternatives in brackets):** exciting (interesting), entertaining (enjoyable), modern (current), excellent (first-rate), gripping (thrilling), dated (old-fashioned), cheap (inexpensive), convenient (user-friendly)

8 **(Suggested answer)**
To conclude, it is my opinion that, despite the advantages videos offer, the cinema will remain in fashion. People will always enjoy an evening of thrilling entertainment away from home.

29 *(Read the rubric and questions aloud. Allow Ss two or three mins. to underline the key words and answer the questions. Check Ss' answers.)*

Key words: advertisement – magazine – child-minder – during school holidays – looking after two children aged 8 & 9 – candidate should be – student aged 16-22 – speak English – free for whole summer – organise children's activities – letter of application to Mrs Miles

1 Formal style, because it is a letter of application to someone you do not know.
2 **(Suggested answer)**
I am writing to apply for – I have some experience of – I am dedicated and reliable – I may be contacted – I look forward to hearing from you soon
3 **(Suggested answer)**
Someone young and energetic, who likes children and is creative.

Revision & Extension Section

30 *(Present the paragraph plan, then allow Ss five or six mins. to read the model and answer the questions. Check Ss' answers.)*

1 To apply for a job as a child-minder (in response to an advertisement)
2 **(Suggested answer)**
   Dear Mrs Miles,
   I am writing in response to your advertisement which appeared in the International Herald on Monday 12th June.
3 Age, nationality, field of study, level of proficiency in English, length of time in England
4 **Qualities to be underlined:** friendly, patient, responsible
   Other qualities: sociable, caring, reliable, etc
5 To show that she has experience in working with children.
6 **(Suggested answer)**
   I feel that I have the qualities and experience necessary to fulfil your requirements. I am available at any time should you wish to meet me.

31 *(Read the rubric and questions aloud. Allow Ss two or three mins. to underline the key words and answer the questions. Check Ss' answers.)*

Key words: private lessons – improve English – advertisement school/college magazine – write a letter – Mrs Daniels – giving information – requesting information in your notes

(Draw Ss' attention to the fact that all notes are important and should be considered as key words.)

1 To ask for information.
2 Formal style, because it is addressed to someone you do not know who holds an official position.
3 Details of yourself and your English studies so far • what you want to practise • why you need to improve your English • cost • where • when • individual or group • teaching material included

32 *(Present the paragraph plan, then allow Ss five or six mins. to read the model and answer the questions. Check Ss' answers.)*

1 The purpose of the letter is mentioned in Para 1
2 • yourself and your English studies so far – Para 2
   • what you want to practise / why you need to improve your English – Para 3
3 • *I feel I need practise in the areas of grammar and conversation in order to improve my accuracy and fluency.*
   • *Furthermore, I am hoping to start a degree course at ..., so the main reason I need Proficiency level English is to enable me to study and socialise there.*
   Linking words/phrases used to express reasons (alternatives in brackets): in order to (to enable me to), which is the main reason (which is why it is important that), to enable me to (so that I can)
4 i) – how much the lessons cost
      – where they take place
      – when they are held
      – whether they are individual or group lessons
      – if all the teaching material is included
   ii) I would appreciate it if ... Could you ... I would be grateful if ...
5 The letter ends with closing remarks and 'Yours sincerely'.
   (Suggested answer)
   Should you require any additional information, please do not hesitate to contact me.
   I look forward to your reply.
   Yours sincerely,
   Erik Sörensen

33 *(Read the rubric and questions aloud. Allow Ss two or three mins. to underline the key words and answer the questions. Check Ss' answers.)*

Key words: short story competition – the story must begin – *I will always remember my first day at ...*

1 **(Suggested answers)**
   at school; at work; etc.
2 First person, because the rubric states you must begin the story *"I will always remember my first day at ..."*
3 Introduction – the place/time, etc in which the story is set
   Main Body – the events of the story in the order they happened
   Conclusion – how the story ended and how you felt

Revision & Extension Section

34 (Present the paragraph plan, then allow Ss four or five mins. to read the model and answer the questions. Check Ss' answers.)

1. a) first day, morning / summer school, London
   b) bright, sunny
   c) my first day at summer school
   (Suggested Introduction)
2. I will always remember my first day at summer school. It was the first time I had ever been away from my home town and I was looking forward to making new friends and seeing new places. So, you can imagine how excited I was that first morning!
3. I was thrilled – feeling very excited – felt as if it was my first day at primary school – I was amazed – Imagine our surprise – I had a great time – a day I will never forget.
4. Past tenses because the story happened some time in the past.
5. The conclusion echoes the opening sentence and explains why it was such a memorable day.

35 (Read the rubric and questions aloud. Allow Ss three or four mins. to underline the key words and answer the questions.)

Key words: short story – magazine for young people – story must begin – *"Don't do that!" I shouted. He ignored me ...*

1. A narrative
2. First person – because the story begins *"Put it down" I shouted. He ignored **me** ...*
3. **(Suggested answers)**
   touching a priceless porcelain vase; tearing a letter of yours; searching your desk; destroying confidential documents; etc

36 a) (Allow Ss five or six mins. to read beginnings and decide which is most suitable. Make sure Ss have understood instructions and explain/ elicit any unknown words.)

(Suggested answer)
B seems to be the best paragraph to begin the story because it gives information on **who** is involved (*writer and John – a student in writer's class*), **where** the story takes place (*in an archaeological museum*), **when** it happens (*on a spring morning*) and **what** happens. The writer has also referred to characters' feelings (*bored, extremely nervous*) and has used direct speech to make the beginning more interesting to the reader.

b) A 4   C 5   E 2   G 3
B 1   D 7   F 6

37 (Allow Ss to read the rubric again and refer them to the paragraph plan on p. 108. Discuss the task and when you are sure Ss understand it, assign as homework.)

(Suggested answer)
... "Put it back where it belongs," I said, but he ignored me and, holding the vase in only one hand, walked towards his friends. I had to stop him before the priceless vase got broken.

To my horror, he tossed the vase into the air and caught it. All his friends laughed and cheered, so he did it again, and again. By now people had gathered round to watch and I had to push my way through the crowd to get to him.

Suddenly, one of his classmates pushed me from behind and I stumbled forward and bumped into John, just as he was tossing the vase into the air again. We both fell to the floor in a heap. Hearing the laughing and cheering from another exhibition room, the curator came running, shouting angrily. He arrived just in time to see John and I falling over and the vase spinning through the air.

He dived and caught the vase before it hit the floor. He was furious. Pointing to the door he shouted at us, "I never want to see any of you here ever again!"

38 (Read the rubric and questions aloud. Allow Ss three or four mins. to underline the key words and answer the questions.)

Key words: working abroad – tour guide – write a letter – friend – describing the job – what you like – what you don't like about the job

1. giving news/information
2. informal, because it is to a friend at home
3. – everyday vocabulary
   – colloquial expressions/idioms/phrasal verbs
   – short forms
4. **(Suggested answers)**
   organising entertainment and sightseeing trips; guiding tourists around famous places, museums, etc; answering tourists' questions

39 (Allow Ss five or six mins. to read the rubric and answer the questions. Explain/Elicit the meaning of any unknown words. Check Ss' answers.)

Revision & Extension Section

1 To give news. The purpose has been stated in the first paragraph. ("... busy ... summer job ... drop you a line and tell you all about it.")

2 **(Suggested answer)**
Well, I've got great news. I started a summer job last month and I love it! Let me tell you all about it.

3 In Para 2. The job involves: looking after people on tours; telling them the history of the places visited

4 **advantage:** meeting people from all over the world
disadvantage: have to get up at 6 am

5 • she has made new friends
• she hates getting up early

6 She asks about her friend's family and tells her to write soon.
(Suggested answer)
My lunch hour is over, so I'd better get back to work! I hope you'll come to London next month so that I can show you around properly!

40 *(Present the paragraph plan, then allow Ss three or four mins. to read the rubric and answer the questions. Check Ss' answers.)*

Key words: work for tourist organisation — university town — large number of foreign students — write a report — eating out in your town — describe best places for students to eat and drink — say why — suitable for foreign students

1 formal style
2 **(Suggested answer)**
fast food restaurants, restaurants, cafés, bars, bistros, etc

41 *(Present the paragraph plan, then allow Ss five or six mins. to read the report and answer the questions. Explain/Elicit the meanings of any unknown words or phrases. Check Ss' answers.)*

1 To provide details of eating and drinking places suitable for students visiting from other countries.
The purpose is clearly stated in the first line of the first paragraph.
The aim of this report is to provide details ...

2 **(Suggested alternative)**
As requested, this report is to provide information on places to eat in the Stonebridge area that would be suitable for foreign students.

3 Points not mentioned: size, decor

4 **(Suggested answer)**
To sum up, foreign students should be well served by the eating and drinking establishments in Stonebridge. They can enjoy good food and entertainment at good value for money in a variety of places.

42 *(Read the rubric and questions aloud. Allow Ss two or three mins. to underline the key words and answer the questions. Check Ss' answers.)*

Key words: A lot of what is taught in school nowadays is not worth learning — teacher — write a composition — with reference to your own learning experiences

1 An opinion essay
2 Opinion essays are usually written in formal or semi-formal style.
3 It means including examples of your own experiences as a student/parent/teacher.
4 *(Ss' own answers)*

43 *(Present the paragraph plan, then allow Ss five or six mins. to read the model and answer the questions. Check Ss' answers.)*

1 Formal
The main characteristics of formal style are:
– formal linking words/phrases: (In the first place; Furthermore; On the other hand; For instance)
– use of the passive (we are taught)
– complex sentences (e.g. without this "background" ... little to me.)

2 The writer disagrees with the statement.
"In my view, the majority of the things we are taught in school are useful to us in many ways."

3 • In the first place, school gives you general knowledge which helps you in your everyday life.
• Furthermore, some school subjects help you develop an interest in hobbies.
• On the other hand, there are some subjects taught in school which seem to me to be a waste of time.

4 Paras 1, 2 and 3 (disagreeing with the rubric)
Para 4 (opposing viewpoint)

5 • My own experience has shown ... would mean very little to me.
• In my case, I like to spend ... Computer Studies at school.
• I particularly dislike ... ever be useful to me.

a) **to list points:** In the first place, Furthermore
b) **to show contrast:** On the other hand, On the contrary
c) **to introduce personal opinion or experience:** In my view, I think, My own experience, In my case, I particularly dislike, I believe that

7 **(Suggested answer)**

In conclusion, although I agree that some subjects taught in schools are not useful in everyday life, the majority of the knowledge we gain during our school years is worthwhile.

44 *(Read the rubric and questions aloud. Allow Ss two or three mins. to underline the key words and answer the questions. Check Ss' answers.)*

Key words: secretary of students' social events committee — write to the principal — asking for permission to have party — plans made so far (information included in Jeff's note)

(Draw Ss' attention to the fact that the notes are important and should all be considered as key words.)

1. The main purpose of the letter is to ask for permission. The two other reasons for writing are: to give information about the organisation of the party and to reassure the principal that there will be no complaints this year.
2. Formal style — because it is to a person in an official position
3. **(Suggested answer)**
   - too much noise / neighbours complained — have party in the college canteen
   - too many people / crowded — ticket holders only (400 maximum)
   - not good music — hire a DJ
   - food ordered from a take away / horrible — students do the cooking

45 *(Present the paragraph plan, then allow Ss five or six mins. to read the model and answer the questions. Check Ss' answers.)*

1. Yes, it is. (I am writing ... to request the use of the college canteen for the summer disco ...)
2. Para 2 — date, time, tickets, music, food and drink, decorations
   Yes, all the details have been included.
3. Para 3 — the writer says that the disco will finish at 11:30pm precisely, committee members will make sure that people leave the building quietly and will tidy and clean all the rooms after the party

4 **(Suggested answer)**

All the students are looking forward to having a celebration to mark the end of a long year of hard work, so we would appreciate it very much if you would give us permission to use the college canteen for the party.

46 *(Allow Ss four or five mins. to read the rubric, underline the key words and answer the questions).*

Key words: You work for a large company — you organise staff social events — write to the director — asking permission to have a party at the office — giving information — organisation of party

(Draw Ss' attention to the fact that the notes are important and should be considered as key words.)

1. The purpose of the letter is to ask permission to hold an office party.
2. Ask permission for office party, reason for party, there won't be complaints this time, date, place, time, food and drink, music and decorations.

47 *(Allow Ss three mins. to read the rubric again and refer them back to the paragraph plan on p. 133. Discuss the task, and when you are sure Ss understand it, assign as HW).*

(Suggested answer)
Dear Mr Franklin,

I am writing on behalf of the staff social committee to request permission to hold a party on the occasion of Sarah Lee's retirement.

We would like to hold the party on 10th May, from 6pm–11pm. We will be inviting Sarah's colleagues from within the company only. No outside guests will attend.

The music will be in the form of tapes and CDs brought in by members of staff. Peter Morris will be organising a buffet and cold drinks while Julie Townsend has kindly offered to decorate the office.

We understand that you may be concerned about the noise level following complaints by local tenants after the Christmas party. However, I can assure you that as this will be a much smaller gathering, there is unlikely to be any kind of disturbance.

I am sure you understand how important Sarah has been to the department and how strongly we feel about honouring her in this way. I therefore hope you will grant us permission to hold the party.

Yours sincerely,
Linda McCloud

Revision & Extension Section

48 *(Read the rubric and questions aloud. Allow Ss two or three mins. to underline the key words and answer the questions. Check Ss' answers).*

Key words: write article – school magazine – suggest helpful ways of remembering new vocabulary in English

1 An essay suggesting solutions to a problem
2 **(Suggested answers)**
    look up words in dictionary; write words in notebook; etc

49 *(Present the paragraph plan, then allow Ss five or six mins. to read the model and answer the questions. Explain/Elicit the meaning of any unknown words. Check Ss' answers around the class).*

1 Here are a few ways to help you remember new vocabulary.
2 Addressing the reader directly/rhetorical question
   (Suggested introduction)
   How often have you spent hours studying lists of new vocabulary only to find you have forgotten most of the words by the next day? Well, don't despair – you aren't alone. Many students have the same problem. I'd like to make a few suggestions which may help to improve your memory.
3 – write each new word on a separate piece of paper and stick them up around your room
   – choose ten words a week to learn and revise regularly
   – use a dictionary
   – use new words in compositions, letters to friends and in conversation
   You will soon learn and build up a good vocabulary.
4 **Expressions used to make suggestions (suitable alternatives in brackets):**
   Here are a few ways to ... (Here are some tips on how to ...)
   One useful method is to ... (One of the best ways to ...)
   It's also a good idea to ... (You could also ...)
   The best way to ... (The most useful method ...)
5 **Words/Phrases to introduce reasons (alternatives in brackets):**
   – In this way (Consequently)
   – By learning (As a result of this)
   – After you have (When you have)
6 To sum up, there are many methods you can use to help you learn vocabulary. But the most important thing to remember is not to give up. If you keep trying, you will succeed!

50 *(Present the paragraph plan, then read the rubric and questions aloud. Allow Ss two or three mins. to underline the key words and answer the questions. Check Ss' answers).*

Key words: jazz festival – which you thought was fantastic – local newspaper report – incorrect – write to editor – correcting the errors – explaining why you think festival should be held again

(Draw Ss' attention to the fact that the article and notes are important and should all be considered as key words).

1 A letter to the editor of a newspaper
2 – to correct errors made in the newspaper report of the festival
   – to explain why you think the festival should be held again

51 *(Allow Ss five or six mins. to read the model and answer the questions. Explain/Elicit the meaning of any unknown vocabulary. Check Ss' answers).*

1 Formal style, because it is a letter to the editor of a newspaper.
2 **(Suggested answer)**
   Dear Sir,
   I am writing to complain about your article on the Farley Music Festival. I would like to draw your attention to several errors that were made.
3 Para 2 – ... *the first band, Magic, were unable to appear at midday as planned*
   Para 3 – ... *performers as second-rate*
   Para 4 – ... *West Wind played for only half an hour*
   Para 5 – ... *"fewer than 2,000" people attended the festival, ...*
   – *"disappointed" ...*
4 **Language used to list points (alternatives in brackets):** First of all (Firstly) – Secondly (What is more) – The third error (Another error) – Finally (Lastly)
5 i) The main point is to give the writer's opinion as to why the festival should be held next year.
   ii) – it provided entertainment for thousands of people
       – it helped trade at local shops
6 **(Suggested answer)**
   I trust that you will take action to correct these errors and ensure that future events are more accurately reported.
   Yours faithfully,
   A L Miller

Revision & Extension Section

52 *(Present the paragraph plan, then read the rubric aloud. Explain/Elicit the meaning of any unknown words, then allow Ss two or three mins. to underline the key words and answer the questions. Check Ss' answers.)*

Key words: magazine for teenagers — story-writing competition — must begin with 'I had dreamed of this moment for years, and now I wanted to show that I deserved the chance' — story

(Suggested answers)

1 First person — because the rubric states 'I had dreamed ...' etc.
2 It should begin with the sentence given in the rubric, because the 'competition rules' say that your story 'must begin' "I had dreamed ...".
3 **(Suggested answers)**
   perform in front of crowd/audience, win an award, being promoted, etc

53 *(Allow Ss three or four mins. to read the text and the questions. Explain/Elicit the meaning of any unknown vocabulary. Ss complete the task. Check Ss' answers, then ask individual Ss to read aloud from the text).*

(Suggested answers)

1 a) the pitch; b) sun shining brightly; c) I was playing for the school football team
2 at last, at first, Then, A minute or two later, after, as, now
3 could hardly believe it, cheering, nervous, began to relax, went wild, proud, feeling pleased, embarrassing, felt like crying, funny, laugh
4 — I ran out onto the pitch.
   — The game began.
   — Jordan headed the ball to me.
   — I passed it to Wesley.
   — He scored.
   — The crowd went wild.
   — I slipped and fell.
   — I had twisted my ankle.
   — The trainer helped me off the pitch.
5 Reference to feelings
6 i) *(Ss' own answers) (Ss, in pairs, think of other ways to end the story.)*

  ii) **(Suggested answer)**
  When it was time for the second half, I was feeling eager to play my best. To my joy, I received a great pass within a couple of minutes of play. I ran with it and beat the defenders to score a perfect goal. I felt good and the crowd started to chant my name.
  At full-time the rest of the team carried me off the pitch on their shoulders. It was the best day of my life.

54 *(Read the rubric and questions aloud, then allow Ss three or four mins. to underline the key words and answer the questions. Check Ss' answers).*

Key words: inventions — your teacher — write a composition — best invention/worst invention in the last 200 years — giving reasons

1 An opinion essay.
2 *(Ss' own answers)*

55 *(Present the paragraph plan, then allow Ss four or five mins. to read the model and the questions. Explain/Elicit the meaning of any unknown vocabulary, then Ss complete the task. Check Ss' answers. Finally, ask individual Ss to read aloud from the text.)*

1 **(Suggested answer)** "All in the name of progress".
2 The article is written in formal style, because it is an opinion essay.
3 **The computer:**
   – can do things we could not do before
   – used in offices/schools/homes
   – important piece of equipment
   – continue to bring new benefits
4 **The motor car**
   – air pollution
   – traffic jams
   – road accidents
5 furthermore, in contrast, However, To sum up, On the other hand
6 **(Suggested introduction)**
   Without a doubt the 20th century has seen many technological advances. Many things have been invented which have had an impact on our daily lives. However, I feel that the modern computer qualifies as the best invention whereas the motor car qualifies as the worst one.

69

Revision & Extension Section

56 *(Present the paragraph plan, then read the rubric and the questions aloud. Allow Ss two or three mins. to underline the key words and answer the questions. Check Ss' answers).*

Key words: announcement — international magazine — teenagers — write an article — My most treasured possession — something of yours that you particularly value — it could be any object, big or small — briefly describe — explain why so important

1 It means something which is very important to you. No, the item doesn't have to be valuable.
2 *(Ss' own answers)*

57 *(Allow Ss five or six mins. to read the model. Explain/Elicit the meanings of any unknown words. Allow Ss a few more mins. to read and answer the questions. Check Ss' answers).*

1 The article is written in semi-formal style — because it is suitable for a teenage magazine.
2 **(Suggested answer)**
    Everyone has something which is important to them. This may be an object which is worth a lot of money, or it may be something which is completely worthless, but which has great sentimental value. My most treasured possession is my personal stereo.
3 Paragraph 2.
4 Para 3 — ... enables me to sit in my room and listen to music ... simply relaxing. The sound doesn't disturb my family and ... when I have got it on.
   Para 4 — ... I can take it everywhere with me/... I never feel bored or lonely.
   (Suggested answer)
   Another reason why I treasure my personal stereo is that I love music and it allows me to listen to music any time I have a few minutes to spare.
5 **(Suggested answer)**
    To conclude, my personal stereo is my most treasured possession because it provides me with entertainment, relaxation and companionship. I take it with me everywhere I go and cannot imagine my life without it.

58 *(Read the rubric and questions aloud. Allow Ss three or four minutes to underline the key words and answer the questions).*

Key words: international magazine for young people — If you were asked to choose an everyday object that has changed our lives — which object would you choose – why? — article

1 An opinion essay
2 **(Suggested answers)**
    mobile phone, TV, CDs, computers, etc
3 *(Ss' own answers)*

59 *(Allow students six or seven mins. to complete the task and make sentences using appropriate linking words/phrases).*

1 D (TV)   3 A (CD)
2 C (computer)   4 B (mobile phone)

(Suggested answers)

- **Firstly**, mobile phones allow us to make calls from anywhere **which** is vital to busy people.
- **What is more**, a computer is an essential tool for business **as** you can access data quickly.
- Television is not only great for entertainment but is also very useful in education. etc

60 *(Allow Ss to read the rubric again and refer them back to the paragraph plan on p. 138. Discuss the task, elicit answers and write them on the board. When you are sure Ss understand it, assign as HW.)*

(Suggested answer)

In my opinion, the object which has changed our lives is the CD. For one thing, it is useful for both computer and music systems, giving us both information and entertainment.
   A CD is a small shiny disk on which sound or data is recorded. It is made of a plastic and is very hard-wearing.
   One reason CDs are especially useful for computer systems is that a lot of information can be stored easily. For example, whole dictionaries and encyclopedias can be stored on them. Furthermore, you can get your information much more quickly.
   Apart from this, CDs provide high quality sound recordings. This makes listening to your favourite band much more satisfying than on records or tapes. Moreover, you can now get CDs which combine the music with the video of the band.
   To sum up, CDs have made our lives simpler and more pleasurable by providing information and entertainment quickly and easily.

61 *(Read the rubric and questions aloud and give Ss two or three minutes to underline the key words and answer the questions).*

Key words: college magazine — write an article — suggesting simple ways for students to keep fit and stay healthy
1 An article giving information.
2 *(Ss' own answers)*
 Suggested answers: go to the gym, go jogging, eat lots of salads, etc.

62 *(Present the paragraph plan, then allow Ss five or six minutes to read the model and answer the questions. Explain/Elicit the meaning of any unknown words. Check Ss answers around the class).*

1 ... there are a number of easy ways to a healthier life.
2 The article is written in a semi-formal style, because it is an article making suggestions (discursive essay).
3 **Suggestions**
 — stop smoking (para 2)
 — get some exercise (para 3)
 — eat healthily (para 4)
4 • The first step is obvious.
 • if you are a smoker, you should stop. (Firstly, people shouldn't smoke.)
 • It is also a good idea to ... (Another useful tip is to)
 • Finally, you should make sure you eat ... (Lastly, try eating)
5 — stop smoking → healthier lifestyle
 — get some exercise → have more energy
 — eat healthily → lose weight, feel better, live longer
6 — The result of (= As a result you would have) giving up smoking
 — If you do this (= Then)
 — As a result (= If you do this)
7 The writer asks a rhetorical question.
 Other techniques (address the reader directly, use a quotation/proverb/saying)
8 **(Suggested answer)**
 So, if you want to lead a longer and healthier life, all you have to do is follow these three easy steps. Start today, after all — what could be simpler?

63 *(Present the paragraph plan, then read the rubric and the questions aloud. Allow Ss two or three mins. to underline the key words and answers the questions. Check Ss' answers).*

Key words: advertisement — local paper — Film Extras Wanted — July — understand English — available for at least a week — full description of yourself — when available — explain why would like job — letter of application

(Draw Ss' attention to the fact that the advertisement is important and should all be regarded as key words).

1 Formal style, because it is a letter of application addressed to someone you don't know.
2 A 'film extra' is a person who appears in the film, but doesn't have a main role, or a speaking part.
3 *(Ss' own answers)*
4 *(Ss' own answers)*

64 *(Allow Ss five or six mins. to read the model and answer the questions. Explain/Elicit the meaning of any unknown words. Check Ss' answers).*

1 The style is formal
 • Advanced vocabulary: (that appeared; attended; I am of average build)
 • Use of would/could: (it would be useful)
 • Use of the passive: (I may be contacted)
 • Formal linking words/phrases (**since** the drama school is)
2 The reason for writing the letter is to apply for the position of film extra. The reason is clearly stated in the first paragraph.
3 **(Suggested answer)**
 Dear Sir/Madam,
 I am writing to apply for the position advertised in last week's edition of The Tribune.
4 • Paragraph 4 includes an explanation of why the writer wants the job.
 • the experience would be useful for her studies and future ambitions.
5 **(Suggested answer)**
 I would be grateful if you could let me know as soon as possible whether I have been chosen for a part in the film, as I need to make the necessary arrangements.
 Yours faithfully,
 Val Fimbres

65 *(Present the paragraph plan, then read the rubric and the questions aloud. Allow Ss two or three mins. to underline the key words and answer the questions. Check Ss' answers).*

Revision & Extension Section

Key words: international music magazine – competition – "Do you prefer live music or recorded music?" – write an article giving your opinion.

1 An opinion essay
2 (Ss' own answers)

66 (Allow Ss four or five mins. to read the model and answer the questions. Explain/Elicit the meaning of any unknown words. Check Ss' answers. Finally, ask individual Ss to read aloud from the text).

1 The writer prefers recorded music.
2 Para 2 – it is more convenient, can listen when and where you want.
  Para 3 – sound quality of CDs, volume to suit yourself
3 **Opposing viewpoint:**
  special atmosphere at a live concert, makes it enjoyable
  – excitement of crowd adds to your own excitement
4 Words/phrases to be underlined (with alternatives)
  To begin with (Firstly)
  Furthermore (In addition)
  What is more (Furthermore)
  On the other hand (Alternatively)
  To sum up (In conclusion)
5 paragraph 4
  (Suggested answer)
  In conclusion, although the last point is undoubtedly true, I am still of the opinion that many people would choose recorded music over live music given the opportunity.

67 (Present the paragraph plan, then read the rubric and the questions aloud. Allow Ss two or three mins. to underline the key words and answer the questions. Check Ss' answers).

Key words: film club – write a report – club chairman – suggesting two films – briefly describe each film – explain why you think club members would enjoy these films

1 A proposal report.
2 The report should be written in a formal style.
3 (Ss' own answers)

68 (Allow Ss five or six mins. to read the model and answer the questions. Explain/Elicit the meaning of any unknown words. Check Ss' answers).

1 Yes, the purpose of the report is clearly stated in the introduction.
  (The purpose of this report is to recommend ...)
  Alternative beginning: The aim of this report is to suggest ...
2 Reasons club members would enjoy the films:
  - both offer a lot to think about
  - amusing and entertaining
  - quality of acting and direction is excellent
3 **(Suggested answer)**
  FIRST RECOMMENDATION
  The Sci-fi epic *The Phantom Menace* continues the Star Wars saga successfully. Liam Neeson and Ewan McGregor star as Jedi Knights performing amazing stunts aided by spectacular special effects.

  SECOND RECOMMENDATION
  You've Got Mail stars two Hollywood favourites, Meg Ryan and Tom Hanks, conducting their courtship over the Internet. This touching and humorous story reaches a predictably happy but satisfying ending.

69 (Allow Ss five or six mins. to read the rubric, underline the key words and answer the questions. Check Ss' answers).

Key words: book club – write a report – club magazine – recommending two books – describe each book briefly – explain why members would enjoy reading them

1 The report should be written in a formal style.
2 (Ss' own answers)
3 – Paragraph 1
  – Paragraphs 2 and 3
  – Paragraph 4

70 (Allow Ss to read the rubric again and refer them to the paragraph plan. Discuss the task and, when you are sure Ss understand the task, assign it as HW.)

(Suggested answer)
To: John Anderson, Club Magazine Editor
From: Lisa Palmer, Book Club Secretary
Subject: Book recommendations
Date: 2nd March, 20...

Aim
The aim of this report is to recommend two books to club members and to suggest reasons why club members would enjoy these books.

72

FIRST RECOMMENDATION
The Pelican Brief by John Grisham is an excellent book. It is a very popular novel about a law student who gets involved in a crime. It is full of mystery and suspense from start to finish.

SECOND RECOMMENDATION
The second recommendation is *The Horse Whisperer* written by Nicholas Evans. The descriptions of the countryside are beautiful and the characters are very realistic, which make it a very moving story.

REASONS FOR RECOMMENDATION
Both books would offer club members good entertainment as well as being thought-provoking. Additionally, both have been made into films, proving that they are great novels. Although both books have different subject matter, both are well-written and entertaining.

CONCLUSION
For the reasons stated above, I can recommend *The Pelican Brief* and *The Horse Whisperer* as my book choices this month. I believe that club members will thoroughly enjoy reading them both.

Unit 2 Informal Letters

➤ **Tapescript for Exercise 1 (p. 20)**

Mother: Jackie!
Jackie: We're in here, Mum!
Mother: Jackie, dear — oh, hello, Sandra! I didn't know you were here ...
Sandra: Hi, Mrs Ebdon.
Mother: Well, I won't disturb you. There's a letter for you, Jackie.
Jackie: Thanks, Mum. ... Oh, great — it's from Monique! You remember her, don't you?
Sandra: Monique — your pen friend from Belgium? Of course I do — I met her when she came to visit you. What does she say?
Jackie: Hang on — let me open it first! ... Okay — she says: "Dear Jackie, Hi — how are you? I hope you're well. Thanks for your last letter, and I'm sorry I've taken so long to write back, but I've been really busy studying. Actually, the reason I'm writing now is to tell you my good news — I passed all my exams with top marks!"
Sandra: That's great! She must be really pleased about that ... What else does she say?
Jackie: She just talks about how worried she was ... dah de dah de dah ... "really important if I want to get into university later" ... hmm hmm hmm hmm ... then she gives some of her results ... she says she got the best marks in her class ...
Sandra: Is that all?
Jackie: I haven't finished reading it yet! Well, she says what she's going to do next ... go on holiday with her parents ... what she plans to study next year ... hmm hmm hmm ... Oh, yes, listen: "Why don't you come and visit me in the summer? I could show you around our city" —
Sandra: Great! Are you going to go?
Jackie: I don't know, Sandra! For a start, I'd have to get Mum and Dad to agree ... Anyway, it's a nice idea ...
Sandra: Does she say anything else?
Jackie: Just about what we can do if I visit. That's all, really. She says: "Well, I'd better end now. Please write back soon and let me know what you think about coming to visit. Give my regards to your mum and dad, and say 'hi' to your friend Sandra. Lots of love, Monique."
Sandra: Ah, she remembers me! You must send her my best wishes when you write back. So — are you going to go and visit her?
Jackie: San-dra! ...
Sandra: Maybe I could come, too! *[fade]* I'd love to go, you know — I've never been to Belgium ...

Unit 3 Formal Letters

➤ **Tapescript for Exercise 1 (p. 26)**

Letter 1

Dear Mr Williams,
  With reference to your advertisement in last week's edition of *Time Out*, I am writing to ask for further information regarding your company's range of products. Firstly, *[fade]* I would be grateful for details of ...
[beep]
... *[fade in]* in reaching a decision about future orders.
  I would greatly appreciate it if you could send me this information as soon as possible. Thank you in advance for your help in this matter.
Yours sincerely,
Robin Jones

Letter 2

Dear Sir/Madam,
  I am writing to express my dissatisfaction with the vacuum cleaner I purchased from your company on 14th June and, in spite of my numerous complaints over the telephone, your failure to send an employee to repair the item.
  Firstly, *[fade]* the appliance was delivered without the accessories ...
[beep]
... *[fade in]* although I was told that the item was covered by a full guarantee.
  As you can imagine, I am extremely upset. I must insist on a full refund or an immediate replacement of the faulty appliance, or I shall be forced to take the matter further.
Yours faithfully,
Brenda Mackie

Letter 3

Dear Sir/Madam,
  I am writing to apply for the position of part-time tour guide which was advertised in today's edition of *Land's End* travel magazine.
I am *[fade]* a 19-year-old student at the local college of ...
[beep]
... *[fade in]* during July and August.
  I may be contacted at the above address, or by telephone on 0181-646-8115. I look forward to hearing from you in due course.
Yours faithfully,
Charles Hinkley

Unit 4 Semi-formal Letters

➤ Tapescript for Exercise 1 (p. 34)

Jackie: Mum!
Mother: Don't shout, Jackie dear — what's the matter, anyway?
Jackie: Mum, can you help me with this letter I'm writing? I've run out of things to say.
Mother: Who are you writing to?
Jackie: To Monique's parents. I want to thank them for having me to stay with them in Belgium, but I don't really know what to put.
Mother: Well, read me what you've written so far.
Jackie: OK ... "Dear Mr and Mrs Clavel, I hope you're fine. I'm just writing to say thanks a lot for putting me up last week. I had a great time —"
Mother: Hold on a minute — you can't write that! It sounds as if you're writing to Monique instead of her parents.
Jackie: So?
Mother: Well, dear, it's not as if they're your best friends. All right, you've known Monique for years, but you don't know her parents very well, do you? You only spent a week with them, and they're much older than you, and ...
Jackie: Yeah, yeah — so what's wrong with what I wrote?
Mother: It's too informal, Jackie ...
Jackie: So what should I put — "I am extremely grateful to you for being so kind", blah blah blah, "I thoroughly enjoyed myself" — that sort of thing?
Mother: No, dear, don't be silly — you don't need to sound quite so official. No, you should be polite, of course, and respectful ...
Jackie: Such as?
Mother: Well, such as, er, you could put ... "I am writing to thank you very much for having me to stay, and to say what a wonderful time I had ..."
Jackie: Oh wait, wait, wait! "... to thank you very much for having me to stay, and to say" — what?
Mother: "What a wonderful time I had." Jackie, I'm *not* going to write the whole letter for you!
Jackie: OK, OK! Give me some ideas, though.
Mother: I don't know, dear — say what you enjoyed about your holiday, tell them about your trip home, things like that. Oh, and don't forget to thank them again at the end of the letter.
Jackie: Mm-hmm — and how do I end the letter? "Lots of love, Jackie"?
Mother: No, dear! I told you — you aren't writing to your best friend.
Jackie: What, then? "Yours faithfully, J M Ebdon"?
Mother: No, dear, of course not — that's for business letters. Put something polite like "Best wishes", and your full name — Jackie Ebdon.
Jackie: OK. Thanks, Mum. I might have to call you for help *[fade]* again if I get stuck, though.

Unit 5 Transactional Letters

➤ Tapescript for Exercise 1 (p. 38)

Dear Sir,

With reference to your advertisement in the April edition of the *Wessex Times*, I am writing to ask for further information regarding the Lynwood Outdoor Centre.

Firstly, I would appreciate it if you could give me a few details concerning the activities offered — for example, whether mountain bikes are available for hire, or if visitors are expected to provide their own. I would also like to know more about the type of area chosen for hiking, and whether a guide accompanies visitors on their hikes.

Furthermore, I would be grateful for information concerning other activities offered at the Centre in addition to those mentioned in your advertisement.

With regard to charges, bookings and so on, I would naturally like to know the total cost of a visit to the centre, and whether visitors are charged by the day, or according to the activities they choose. Finally, could you tell me whether it is advisable to book beforehand?

I look forward to hearing from you in due course, at the address above or by telephone on 0181-313-9480. Thank you in advance.
Yours faithfully,
Michael Williams

Unit 6 Describing People

➤ Tapescript for Exercise 1a (p. 42)

Mum: So ... how was your first week back at school, then, Danny? Made any new friends?
Danny: A few — but my best friends are still Alex, Ravi and Martin.
Mum: Weren't they in your class last year?
Danny: Yeah — we've been put together again this year.
Mum: Well, you sound as if you all get on okay. Why don't you invite them round some time?
Danny: Can I? You'd love Ravi. His parents are from India. He's tall and slim and he's got black hair. He's a bit quiet, though ... well, he doesn't talk very much, but he's really sporty. He's on all the school sports teams and he's the best footballer in our year.

Mum: So, are Alex and Martin good at sport as well?
Danny: They're okay — but not as good as Ravi. Alex is too short to play basketball and he's a bit chubby, so he can't run very fast.
Mum: So why do you like him so much?
Danny: Alex is really funny — he's always playing jokes on everybody and being told off for messing about in class. Old Dobson goes mad!
Mum: He sounds a bit naughty.
Danny: Yeah, Alex *can* be naughty now and then.
Mum: Well — I just hope he doesn't get you into trouble, that's all!
Danny: Not me! It's poor Martin who gets all the blame, because he looks a bit like Alex. I mean, he's taller and thinner, but his face is a lot like Alex's — same nose and rosy cheeks. So teachers sometimes mistake him for Alex.
Mum: That's not fair!
Danny: I know. Martin's really well-behaved as well. He always does his homework and gets good marks in everything. Martin's the clever one!
Mum: Well — they all sound a lot of fun. Why don't you tell them to come round and play on the computer tomorrow?
Danny: Really, Mum? Brilliant! Thanks!

Unit 7 Describing Places/Buildings

➤ Tapescript for Exercise 1 (p. 48)

Tom: Hello, Amy — I haven't seen you for a while! What've you been up to?
Amy: Actually, I've just got back from Buenos Aires.
Tom: Buenos Aires — mm — that's in Argentina, isn't it?
Amy: Yes, it's the capital. It's on the north-east coast, in a really beautiful part of the country, near the Rio de la Plata.
Tom: Oh, lucky you! So, mm ... is there much to see there? What are the main tourist attractions like?
Amy: Oh, there's loads to see and do. The day after I arrived, I went on an organised tour of the city. We started in the Plaza de Mayo, where most of the main sights are. We went into the Metropolitan Cathedral first ... that was really magnificent ... anyway, then we went across the square to watch the changing of the guard outside the Casa Rosada.
Tom: Casa Rosada, eh? What's that, then?
Amy: Well, it's Spanish for "pink house" — it's where the President lives.
Tom: It's not really pink, though, is it?
Amy: Yes, it *is*, honest! Actually, it's a really beautiful building.
Tom: So, did you go inside this, mm, Casa Rosada?
Amy: Well, we went into the Visitor's Museum, but we weren't allowed into the house itself.
Tom: And did you do any shopping while you were there?
Amy: Of course! There are loads of markets and fairs to go to in Buenos Aires — like the antiques fair on Sundays ...
Tom: Antiques?
Amy: Mm-hmm ... and a really big market at San Telmo, which was great for bargains. I bought some really nice presents there.
Tom: Oh, where's *my* present then?
Amy: Oh ... well ... I just bought things for my family, you know ...
Tom: It's okay, I'm only joking! So tell me about the evenings — was there much to do, or were you exhausted after all your other activities?
Amy: Well, I must say it was good just relaxing a bit in the early evening. We went to the cinema once or twice, but most nights we'd sit in the square, drinking coffee and watching the world go by. Afterwards we usually had dinner somewhere nearby — there were hundreds of restaurants to choose from.
Tom: Did you like the Argentinian food?
Amy: Yeah, it was delicious. There's a big variety, too. We even went to a Russian restaurant one evening — you can find almost any kind of food you want in Buenos Aires. It's amazing!
Tom: It sounds like you had a really nice time there.
Amy: Oh, I did — I really enjoyed myself. I'm really glad I went there. If you ever have the opportunity to visit the city, I'd definitely recommend it.

➤ Tapescript for Exercise 9a (p. 51)

Presenter: For our first programme on historic British buildings, what could be more suitable than Buckingham Palace, the home of the royal family? Buckingham Palace is located in central London, close to Hyde Park, and it's a building which is sure to impress you.

The Palace was built in the eighteenth century, but has had many buildings added to it since then. It didn't actually become the royal family's official home until 1850.

The front part of the building is made of grey marble and is on four levels. It has very large windows, and a huge balcony at the front, where the royal family greet the crowds on special occasions. There is a magnificent garden with a small lake at the back of the palace, surrounded by high walls and tall iron railings.

The interior of Buckingham Palace can now be seen by the public and is luxuriously decorated. Altogether, the palace has 600 rooms, and three miles of red carpets cover the floors. The rooms are large and spacious and are filled with valuable antiques, as well as priceless paintings that have been passed down through generations of kings and queens of England.

All in all, Buckingham Palace is a really fascinating building that should certainly not be missed by any visitor to London.

Unit 8 Describing Objects

➢ Tapescript for Exercise 1 (p. 54)

A: Good morning — London Underground Lost Property Office. Can I help you?
B: Yes, er, good morning ... er, I'd like to report a missing suitcase, please.
A: Just a minute while I get the form, sir. Right, here we are. Your name, sir?
B: White, John White.
A: And your address and phone number?
B: 25, Central Road, Camden Town — oh, and my phone number is 773-0502.
A: Where and when did you last see your suitcase, sir?
B: Er, last night. On the underground. I, er, I left it on the tube from Heathrow. It was late, you see — about 11.30 — and there was no one I could report it to. Ah, um, a guard told me to call you first thing this morning.
A: I see. Let me just write that down — 11.30 pm ... and yesterday was ... let's see ... 5th November. Okay — now, can you describe your suitcase for me, please?
B: Oh — er — oh, yes, well it's, er, quite large ... and it's grey — er — dark grey.
A: Well, we do get a lot of large grey suitcases handed in, sir. What's it made of?
B: Er, plastic, I think ... yes, a, er — quite a hard plastic.
A: I see, sir. Is there anything else that would help us identify it? Has it got wheels or anything like that?
B: Er ... no, but it does have a few brightly-coloured stickers on it — I travel quite a lot, you see.
A: Stickers ... Okay, sir, I've made a note of that. Could you describe the contents for me, please — in detail, if possible?
B: Mm — let me think ... er ... what did I put in there? Mmm ... clothes, and, er ... presents and, er, oh dear, lots of things ...
A: Perhaps, sir, if you could make a list and call back — or better still, pop into the office to complete the form?
B: Oh, yes, I could do that ... erm ... er ... *[fade]* what time do you close?

Unit 9 Describing Festivals/Events/Celebrations

➢ Tapescript for Exercise 1 (p. 56)

A: ... talking of holidays, have you decided where you're going this year?
B: Well, I was thinking of going to Spain.
A: Oh, I went there last year.
B: Really? Whereabouts?
A: Barcelona — oh, there was a brilliant festival on when I was there.
B: A festival? What was it called?
A: "La Mercé", I think. Anyway, it lasted for about four days.
B: When was that, then?
A: Um, let me think ... it must have been at the end of September.
B: So, is there any special reason for this festival?
A: Well, the Spanish don't really need to have a reason for a festival, but this one celebrates the patron saint of Barcelona.
B: And it lasts for *four days*? That must take a lot of preparation.
A: Yes, it does. The locals told me they start preparing for it well in advance.
B: So what sort of things do they have to do beforehand?
A: Well, I know they start making costumes for the parade months before the event. And the local musicians have to practise a lot, to get ready for their performances during the festival.
B: And what was the actual festival like last year? I mean, what kind of events did they have?
A: Oh, all sorts. As I said, there was live music, with bands in all the main squares, and people were dancing a lot, too, mainly "Sardanas" — the traditional dance from that part of Spain.
B: What else?
A: Er, let's see ... well, there were lots of parades, but the main one is called "Carrefoc," where people dress up as monsters and dragons. Oh, and the acrobats! ...
B: What about the acrobats?
A: There were these acrobats performing ... they did some amazing tricks!
B: Well, it all sounds very entertaining ...
A: Yes — and the last night of the festival was the best. They lit up a fountain in the main square with beautiful coloured lights. Then suddenly the music stopped and all the lights in the square went out.
B: What happened? Was it a power cut?
A: No! We all held sparklers and there was a huge firework display.
B: Oh, I see!

Tapescripts

A: Yes ... it was really spectacular.
B: Sounds fantastic! I think I'll book my holiday for September and make sure I'm in Barcelona for the festival.
A: Well, you won't regret it, I promise you.
B: [fade] I'll go and ring the travel agents now ...

➤ Tapescript for Exercise 7 (p. 59)

Lorna: Yeah, and did I tell you it was my parents' silver wedding anniversary last Saturday?
Katie: Silver — wow! Does that mean they've been married 50 years?
Lorna: No — that's a golden wedding anniversary! They're not *that* old yet, Katie! Silver is the 25th wedding anniversary!
Katie: Oh, yeah, I remember now, ha! ha! Well ... how did they celebrate it?
Lorna: Actually, my brother and I organised a big surprise party for them. We hired a reception room at the Regent Hotel — you know, the new one on the seafront.
Katie: That must have taken quite a bit of organising!
Lorna: Well, I suppose it *was* a lot of work — but it was worth it.
Katie: What sort of things did you have to do?
Lorna: Well, we sent out all the invitations weeks in advance. Also, some relatives were coming from abroad, so we had to book rooms for them.
Katie: Wasn't that expensive?
Lorna: No, not really ... the Regent gave us a discount for the rooms — you know, because we were having the party there.
Katie: That's good. Did you have to hire caterers, too?
Lorna: No, the hotel gave us some menus to choose from. We also ordered flower arrangements to decorate each table. I chose peach roses, because that's what Mum had in her bridal bouquet when she got married.
Katie: Oh, how lovely! Well, with all that planning the party must have been a great success.
Lorna: Yes, it was. Almost everyone we'd invited came along. There were about 50 people in the end! The evening began with a really delicious three-course meal. Everyone said how much they enjoyed it. Then, later on, we all got up and danced.
Katie: So what kind of music did they play?
Lorna: Oh, mostly Sixties numbers my parents knew — the Beatles and that sort of thing. I've never seen my dad dance so much!
Katie: Yuk — Sixties — ahh — not my kind of thing, I'm afraid. Anything else interesting happen at the party?
Lorna: Well, Mum was in tears most of the evening, hugging and kissing long-lost relatives. But the highlight of the evening was when Uncle Ron got up and made a funny speech about how Mum and Dad met.

Katie: Well, it sounds like your parents had a wonderful time — that's the main thing.
Lorna: They certainly did. Mum said the best thing was having all her family together, for once. In fact, she's already planning the guest list for their 30th anniversary!
Katie: Oh, dear — need some help with the preparations?
Lorna: Yes, please!

Unit 10 Stories - First Person Narratives

➤ Tapescript for Exercise 1 (p. 60)

Narrator: I will always remember the day I took my driving test. It was a cold, misty February morning and the clouds that covered the sky like a dreary grey blanket didn't help to calm my anxiety. I made myself a cup of tea, but I couldn't bring myself to eat anything.

My instructor arrived. Seeing my nervous expression, she smiled. "Relax," she said. "It's only a driving test." We got into her shiny new Corsa and set off for our last lesson. I didn't do too badly, but I couldn't shake off my nervousness. We went to the test centre and I became more and more anxious as I sat waiting for my turn. The examiner finally arrived and as he and I got into the Corsa, I felt sick with fear.

We hadn't travelled very far when the examiner asked me to park in the space between two parked cars. My heart was pounding in my chest and my palms were sweating so much that they kept slipping off the wheel. My knees were shaking, and I could hardly manage to keep my foot on the pedal. Suddenly, I pressed the accelerator too hard and the car shot forward. There was a sickening crunch as I bashed into the car in front of me. My heart jumped into my mouth. Then, in my panic, I made matters worse by putting the car into reverse and slamming into the car behind, too. Again, I heard the sound of breaking glass and crunching metal. I wanted the ground to open up and swallow me. The examiner was screaming hysterically, "Stop, Mr Wainwright, stop! Don't do anything else!"

Needless to say, I failed the test. Fortunately, the two cars I hit only needed minor repairs, and that was covered by the insurance. However, my instructor's car was so badly damaged that it had to be towed away. She was furious.

After that, I bought a bike. Well, it may not be the safest thing for me, but it's cheaper and it's certainly a lot safer for the other drivers!

> **Tapescript for Exercise 6a (p. 62)**

Picture A

Narrator: The moon was beautiful, like a diamond set in deep blue velvet. Occasionally, I heard the sound of loud car horns and noisy shouting. I looked at the calm water of the bay far below, reflecting the sparkling lights of tall buildings and tiny boats.

Picture B

Narrator: There was a hot, humid atmosphere in the forest. The summer sun filtered through the shiny green leaves, and the air was filled with the smell of damp ferns.

Picture D

Narrator: I couldn't hear anything but the roar of the sea and the waves thundering and crashing on the rocks. I was amazed by the power of the white foamy water. The wind blew fiercely through my hair and my face was soon wet from salty sea spray.

Unit 11 Stories - Third Person Narratives

> **Tapescript for Exercise 1 (p. 66)**

Narrator: Jeff woke up with a shock and realised he was late. He got dressed and rushed out into the busy main road to get a taxi. He was desperate to reach the airport in time for his flight, so when a taxi stopped further up the street, Jeff raced towards it.

When he reached the taxi, an elderly white-haired man was just about to climb into it. Jeff pushed past him, shouted "Sorry, but I'm in a hurry!" and jumped into the taxi. He slammed the door shut and the taxi drove away, leaving the old man standing on the pavement. Jeff reached the airport just in time for his flight and heaved a sigh of relief as he sat down in his seat by the window.

He felt rather annoyed when the captain announced there would be a slight delay, as a passenger had checked in late.

Jeff was reading his newspaper when the late arrival finally boarded the plane and sat in the seat next to him. As Jeff lowered his paper to greet the stranger he was so embarrassed that he went as red as a beetroot. Sitting next to him was the elderly white-haired man whose taxi he had stolen earlier that morning.

Unit 12a News Reports

> **Tapescript for Exercise 1a (p. 72)**

Newsreader: And now, let's take a closer look at today's main stories. Local people on the island of St. Finn are protesting about the Pepco Petroleum Company's failure to take prompt action over an oil spill on Tuesday night from one of their tankers.

The Ocean Triton hit a group of rocks off the coast of St. Finn, ripping a hole in the vessel. Tons of oil have since leaked from the tanker, creating an oil slick which has covered much of the island's east coast, harming seabirds and other wildlife in the area.

A clean-up operation is in progress to rescue injured seabirds and the local council has begun to clean up the beaches. However, it seems that little can be done about the fish stocks destroyed by the spill.

Angry residents are now counting the cost of the incident in terms of the ecological damage. A council spokesman commented: "It is not the first time that we have faced a situation like this, but it is one of the worst." Pepco's spokesperson, however, was unavailable for comment.

News is coming in *[fade]* about a pile-up on the M11 motorway earlier this morning ...

Unit 13 "For and Against" Essays

> **Tapescript for Exercise 1 (p. 82)**

Sue: So, what do you fancy for dinner tonight, then?
Ron: Actually, I'm tired of eating in. Why don't we go out for a change?
Sue: Are you trying to say that you don't like my cooking?
Ron: Of course not — you're a fantastic cook! It's just that it's fun to eat out now and again. It's nice to have someone else to do all the work for a change, don't you think?
Sue: Well, I must admit, it's not as tiring as cooking after a hard day at the office. Okay, then, where do you suggest?
Ron: You know, I've been dying to try that new pizzeria on the High Street.
Sue: Oh, I'm not sure. I've heard their pizzas are frozen. I prefer to make my own — at least they're fresh. Most of the restaurants around here are the same — they all use frozen food.
Ron: Okay, let's go to the city centre — somewhere more upmarket. I haven't been to the Shalimar for ages, and you have to admit the food is good.
Sue: Yes, but it's also very expensive! I can make a curry that's just as good for half the price. Now, where's that Indian cookbook? Er ...
Ron: Alright, then — how about fish and chips at Harry's Diner? Ha! He's cheap enough.
Sue: Yuk — no thanks! The last time I ate there the food was swimming in oil, and Harry puts far too much salt on everything. It's very unhealthy, you know.

Ron: I know! Why don't I cook for a change? I bought some fresh vegetables at the market this morning ...
Sue: Now you're talking! Mmm, you could make us a nice vegetable curry, hm ... ?

Unit 14a Opinion Essays

➤ Tapescript for Exercise 1 (p. 88)

Teacher: So, now we've discussed the article, I'd like to hear your views. First of all, Donna, what do you think about free health care?
Donna: Well, I believe it's a basic human right.
Teacher: Could you say why?
Donna: Well, because everyone deserves free medical treatment when they're ill.
Teacher: Ricky – do you agree?
Ricky: Yeah – that would be okay if there was enough money to pay for everyone, but there isn't. I think people who can afford it should pay for their treatment.
Donna: Oh, is that fair?
Ricky: Well, I think so, because in that way more money could be spent on treating those who really need it.
Donna: Mmm, I can see what you mean, but you know, maybe health care wouldn't be such a problem if the government spent more time and money on health education.
Ricky: So how would that help, then?
Donna: Well, more people would learn to have healthier lifestyles, so fewer people would get ill.
Ricky: I'm not so sure about that ...
Teacher: Well, some good points there. Thank you, Donna and Ricky. Now let's see what the others think. Yes, Julie ...

Unit 15 Assessment & Proposal Reports

➤ Tapescript for Exercise 1 (p. 102)

A: Good morning, Mr and Mrs Dakin. Are you enjoying your stay here at Oaklands?
Mrs D: Oh, we're having a lovely time, thank you.
A: Good, good. I was wondering if perhaps you could fill in this questionnaire before you leave. It's to help us see what we need to improve at Oaklands Health Farm.
Mrs D: Oh, we'd be happy to.
A: Great! Well, I must be off now – take your time with the questionnaire, *[fade]* there's no rush ...
Mrs D: Why don't we fill this in now – my exercise class isn't for another half an hour. Let's see ... 'Location'. Well, it's only an hour from London by car, which is good ...
Mr D: Yes, but not everyone lives in London, and if you don't have your own car it's probably quite difficult to get here ... the nearest station is at least twenty minutes away. Shall I tick 'Average'?
Mrs D: 'Average'. Okay. Now, what about 'Facilities'?
Mr D: Oh, there's no doubt about it, Oaklands' facilities are outstanding. There are tennis courts, beautiful large bedrooms, a swimming pool ... What else could you ask for? I'll tick 'Excellent'.
Mrs D: Hang on a minute! What about the gym? Some of the equipment in there doesn't even work – and you have to book the tennis courts the day before you want to play! I think we should tick 'Good'.
Mr D: Yes, maybe you're right. Let's put 'Good' then. Okay, next is 'Treatments'. You know more about that than me, you seem to have had every beauty treatment available!
Mrs D: Ha, ha, very funny. Anyway, it's only because there are so many on offer, I had to try them all!
Mr D: Are they any good, then?
Mrs D: Yes, there's a huge choice and they're all wonderful. Yesterday I had a foot massage and today I'm going to have a seaweed wrap – it's supposed to help you lose weight ...
Mr D: Yuck! I'll put 'Excellent', then, shall I?
Mrs D: Yes, definitely. What's next? Ah – 'Food'.
Mr D: Food – my speciality! Actually, the food hasn't been as good as I expected it to be. I've found it rather boring and tasteless.
Mrs D: Darling, that's because all the dishes on the menu are low in fat. They're very healthy and good for you. Mind you, I do wish there were more puddings to choose from ... I'm getting a bit sick of fruit salad every day.
Mr D: So am I! I still think the main courses could be nicer, too, so, mmm, let's put 'Average'.
Mrs D: Yes, I agree, put 'Average'.
Mr D: Now, there's a space here for 'General Comments'. What shall we say?
Mrs D: Let me think ... Okay, let's put "Oaklands' facilities are very good ..."
Mr D: Wait a moment ... "very good." All right, go on.
Mrs D: "There is also an excellent range of treatments available ..." What else?
Mr D: "The food at Oaklands is rather disappointing, and the menu could be improved. Overall, though, our stay at Oaklands has been enjoyable and we will be recommending it to our friends." There, that's enough isn't it?
Mrs D: Yes, that's fine. Oh, look, we haven't ticked 'Poor' for any of the questions.
Mr D: Well, that just shows how pleased we are with Oaklands, doesn't it?